Contents

I. Introduction

The idea that 'the world is a stage', and the theatre a 'mirror of the world' exists in many languages and is probably as old as the theatre itself.

The Greek word *theatron* indicated the place where portrayals took place, where one 'looked on with amazement' and where public spectacles were performed. In English, according to the Oxford Dictionary, *theatre* means 'a place for viewing dramatic plays or other spectacles; a playhouse', and 'the scene of action, a thing displayed to view, a spectacle'. One would speak of individual pieces written for the theatre as dramas or plays. On the other hand, referring to the theatrical productions of a country or continent, the term 'theatre' would again be used (as in Senegalese theatre, African or American theatre) but 'drama' would refer to an individual play.

In this book the meaning of the word is quite comprehensive. The origin of the theatre is difficult to determine, because we do not have enough information to determine exactly when theatre began and how it developed in human society. It is thought that dramatic forms often developed from religious rites, since there are examples which seem to have resulted from such an evolution.

The history of the Greek word *drama* is interesting. This term, signifying 'action', was used for the first time in the sense of 'dramatic action' in 560 B.C. by a Greek called Thespis when he introduced a costumed and masked performer to the songs and dances in his religious choirs. This character represented one part of the action in speech and gestures. After that the term *drama* came to indicate artistic labour, expressing in imaginary fashion an event before a public and making use of one or several artists. It took on the meaning of an event in which the action centres around humanity.

Dramatic expression can serve to order and to control society, to ensure the survival of the species. It can also modify and influence society. In the dance the mimicking of the movements of an animal comes from the belief that the dancer thereby brings the animal to submission. There are also sowing, harvesting, rain, war, fertility and death dances. The dance is not only a ritual, but also a labour, a meaningful action, leading to a required result.[1] Hunninger[2] suggests that originally in the 'creation of a world order' gesture have played a more important role than language. This is so because of the emotional and collective nature of the ritual. Language might be inadequate when expressing matters of life and death. In the ritual, however, the importance of gestures and of words evolves differently from one region to another — depending on whether they are danced, sung or spoken. Rituals have to be executed to perfection. One mistake or omission destroys the desired effect and requires that they be repeated. Magic rituals without dramatic actions are difficult to imagine. Nevertheless theatre in the real sense of the term did not begin before there was a division into two groups, where 'the movement encounters an opposing movement . . . where one coryphee detaches himself from the chorus, and not only leaves the chorus, but takes up a position in opposition to them'.[3]

Originally no one remained outside the event. Each one played his role, though some roles were more important than others. Only with the passing of time did forms develop where dramatic roles were attributed solely to certain people, while the other participants became the audience. It can also be supposed that when the group became too large a small number eventually represented the entire community during the ritual event. But all of this must be seen as hypothesis rather than verifiable fact.

There are also the very ancient plays the purpose of which was to divert death or evil; a kind of early ritual sacrifice to save the community. In modern and ancient theatre the theme of the individual sacrificing himself for a group is sometimes found. In Africa the playwright Wole Soyinka made use of it in his play *The Strong Breed* (1963).

In a society that is considered archaic, the myth constitutes the charter for communal life and culture. According to Eliade[4] myth tells sacred history and conveys the absolute truth on which all human actions should be based:

The myth is *real* and *sacred*, so it becomes an *example* and consequently repeatable, for it serves as a model,

and also a justification for all human actions. In other
terms a myth is *true history* which took place at the
beginning of time and which is the model for human
action.

More recent literature places less emphasis on the
historic core of myth. Claude Lévy-Strauss[5] for
example interprets myth more as an expression of a
cosmology. The symbolism of the myth hides a
message: to overcome conflict, such as that between
god and man, between man and woman or between
man and animal. Often myths are concerned with the
relationship between nature and culture.

Myths do not only ensure continuity, they also
stabilize the internal relationships of a society. For
that reason the exemplary prowess of a god or a
mythological hero is portrayed or their adventures
related. Imitation and narration are part of the ritual
play, which ensures the cycle of life. It can be seen
that the drama developed from this kind of theatre,
when one or more dancers, singers or actors detach
themselves from the group and play their own roles;
the drama of life or death, of a sacred animal, a god, a
spirit or a hero. So we must have movement and
counter-movement, action and reaction, actors and
audience. The actor is the coryphee, 'the interpreter
of that which moves the community in the literal
sense of the word'.[6] The dancers, who are also the
actors, often wear masks in pantomime. In Africa as
elsewhere masks have a long history. They are used in
ceremonies the function of which is to ensure the
unity of the group. In masquerades dance and music
alternate with song and the recitation of mythical
poetry. Such ceremonies can last for days. Most often
the men wear masks which the women are not even

allowed to see. There are also ceremonies to which women alone have access.[7] The one who wears the mask symbolizes the history of ancient times, thereby demonstrating a unity between the past and the existing community. When they wear masks the actors become links in the chain which joins the common man to the mythical world of the gods, spirits and heroes. The mask asserts the reality of the myth in everyday life and the continuity of traditional values in society.

Masks are used in many ceremonies. During initiation the leader wears one when he represents the spirit which teaches men the art of living. Often initiation ends with masked dances which express its meaning, the adolescent 'dying of his childhood'[8] and being reborn as an adult. Ceremonial masks also serve to protect the society against crime and sorcery, but they can be put to anti-social uses. Often secret societies, like the leopard men in Zaire, have masks which are worn at ritualistic reunions. Masks protect dancers during a ritual, e.g. when the life-force liberated by the death of a man or an animal is seized by the dancers. The effects of such forces cannot be evil as long as they are used for the benefit of the community. In sacred acts, which originally constituted the drama, the mask was an instrument of magic that could make life triumph over the forces opposed to it[9] and that ensured contact with the mythical world.

The most ancient literature was transmitted orally from one generation to another. The myths and legends, the ancestral history, the wanderings of peoples and the deeds of great chiefs were preserved in human memory without having been reduced to writing.

In oral literature the portrayal is dominant whereas in written literature the text is everything. This text is permanent, even though different readers might interpret it, each in his own way. During the narration of ancient stories speech or song might be used. Music, dance, song, mime, masks and costumes form a unique unity. The narrator improvises on known themes, although the portrayal as a whole unfolds in the traditional frame of ritual actions, formulae and refrains. The purpose of the narration is again the revival of the myth.

Van der Leeuw[10] emphasises the presence of comic elements in the ritual portrayal, which he refers to as 'sacral'. The dramatic action was originally a unity where the serious and the comic were not separated. Liturgy and farce were joined in the same context. The fertility of man, animal and plant is always the central theme, rite and fertility having a very close relationship.

Besides ritualistic portrayals other forms developed. The initial unity did not then exist. Hunninger[11] explains how he sees the evolution of the very ancient rituals leading to tragedy and comedy in Greece. In other societies the drama evolved along comparable lines.

The success of poetry and theatre depends to a large extent on the talents of narrators and actors. In Europe during the middle ages when they visited the courts and chateaux with their one-man shows, they were called bards, minstrels or troubadours. In the streets mimes and clowns acted out their farces, buffooneries and fables, while public worship in the middle ages was represented by mysteries and passion plays.

The *commedia dell'arte* had considerable influence

on the popular theatre in Europe and especially in France. In it there were traditional figures who were easily recognizable by the people because of their masks, costumes and stylized gestures. The plays were improvised and employed simple theatrical effects. The text was only one element among many others. Song, dance, pantomime, acrobatics and décor all had roles.[12] This folk theatre preserved all of its vitality even after comedy, tragedy and modern theatre had been developed and the public had been reduced to the role of the passive and silent audience. Today, in western society, there is not much left of such rituals in which the entire community is involved.

The essence of our human conduct is being hidden more and more in the margin of modern existence, where the theatre is also found. It appears, however, that we are gradually becoming aware of the fact that the history of man is not an immutable evolution from 'primitive' man to 'modern western man', but that the myth remains one of the deepest elements of our being.[13] Perhaps this realization can explain the number of attempts in Europe and America at rediscovering dramatic forms which go back to ancient rites.

The major aspects touched on so far imply that development and change in a society leads to other forms of dramatic expression. In a global (non-differentiating) society the whole group participates in the ritual play. The differentiation can be noted in theatre as well as in many other areas when the religious is separated from the temporal and the tragic from the comic. At all times the theatre is a mirror of human existence.

If the African theatre today 'reflects' several

periods at the same time, it is because of the simultaneous existence of many different kinds of communities. We shall return to this in the following chapters with the description of the oral and dramatic traditions which existed in Africa before it came into contact with the West.

At that stage we shall see how the oral tradition, in form as well as theme, constitutes a source of inspiration to the modern African dramatist. Despite this he may be influenced to a certain extent by western theatre. Finally in the following three chapters three important themes which form the subject matter of works by most playwrights will be discussed. They are colonialism, the movement away from a traditional society and urbanisation. These themes have direct relevance to contemporary African society.

A book about the theatre and society in Africa would be incomplete if Wole Soyinka did not figure in it. Because of the scope and the particular qualities of his work, but also in view of his searching social criticism, he will be the object of a separate analysis. His work is sometimes difficult to grasp, but after the preliminary discussion of traditional forms and the three themes mentioned, the many elements of his work will be more accessible to the reader.

The theatre does not 'reflect' society in an objective manner. An objective reality does not really exist. The theatre is an instrument by which dancers, singers, narrators, writers and actors interpret their own idea of reality.

FOOTNOTES:

1. cf Benedict 1935, p 66.
2. 1955, p 16.
3. Van der Leeuw 1955, p 86.
4. 1957, pp 21 ff.
5. 1958, 1964 — 1971.
6. Van der Leeuw 1955, p 85.
7. Laude 1972, p 200, Eliade 1957, 262 ff.
8. Senghor 1964, p 201.
9. Laude 1972, pp 197 ff, Hunninger 1966, pp 23 ff.
10. 1955, pp 91, 92.
11. 1955, pp 29 ff.
12. Voltz 1964, p 40.
13. Eliade 1957, pp 38, 39.

II. Oral Literature
and Total Theatre

It is unrealistic to make a clear division between oral literature and theatre. Oral literature is always theatre, because the way in which the subject matter is performed is an essential aspect of the art.

Theatre and traditional oral literature always recreate the original work.[1] Feelings, mimicry, gestures, intonation, the use of rhythms and pauses, variations in the emotions expressed, the immediate reactions of the actors towards the audience and vice versa: this is all part of the oral character of unwritten African literature and is in fact inherent in the theatre.

Ruth Finnegan[2] emphasizes the fact that in the study of oral literature its most fundamental characteristic has been overlooked. The significance of the performance itself and the essential presence of the performers without whom it cannot exist as a 'literary product' are often forgotten. That 'real theatre' did not exist in pre-colonial Africa is an example of western ethnocentric thinking. It is false to take western theatre as it has developed during recent centuries as a criterion to determine whether or not the theatre exists among other peoples. In Europe the verbal element has finally dominated all other aspects in drama. Elsewhere this is not necessarily the case: the word may be subservient to other elements or form a harmonious unity with them. Of course, this does not mean that they have no dramatic forms of their own. In both cases it is a question of the norms of the society in which those forms developed. Van der Leeuw's wide definition makes it possible to avoid this kind of sterile discussion. Moreover, during the thirties, Antonin Artaud had already attacked the purely verbal and psychological character of western theatre. In *Le théâtre et son double*, written in 1934, he accuses the West of having prostituted the theatre:

> Why is it that in the theatre, at least in the theatre as we know it in Europe, for that matter in the West, everything that is specifically theatrical, i.e. everything that doesn't obey expression by speech, by words, or if you wish everything that isn't contained in dialogue . . . is left in the background?

For that reason Artaud became deeply involved in the Eastern theatre, which uses forms that are not merely verbal. This multiplicity of facets allows the Eastern theatre to retain a character that is concrete, spatial and total.

Oral African literature does not exist without dramatic expression. The performance, the presentation, is a total event in which all those present take part, whether by narrating or making music, by clapping in rhythm or by dancing or singing refrains. Throughout the performance there are favourable or unfavourable reactions, the spectators functioning as immediate critics. Everyone is closely involved in the performance. The narrator is usually poet, singer, narrator and actor at the same time. He is a poet because he recreates the handed-down 'texts' in his own way by improvising on the basis of his knowledge of his art and his control of traditional literature.[3] He is a singer because he sings the text either wholly or partially, and a musician because he accompanies himself on an instrument. There is often a complete orchestra of percussion instruments; drums, xylophones and the like. He is an actor because he interprets the different roles with voice and gesture.

Then there is the active role that the public plays. The dancing, music and song have a communal character and consist of a dialogue between two groups or between individuals and a group. Today dancing and music are still vital to African theatre. This is true even of the work of those African dramatists who have been influenced by the West.

THE TRADITIONAL NARRATOR

The term *narrator* is used for the lack of a better word. The point has already been made that the African oral narrator has to be versatile. In French the term *griot* is used, which according to Eno-Belinga[4] is derived from the Wolof word *gewel* and from the word *dyeli* in Bambara. Eno-Belinga is also of the opinion that African myth, epic and poetry cannot be studied seriously if divorced from the interpreter.

Both professional and amateur narrators exist. The professionals can be divided into those who are itinerant and those who are settled, the latter being permanently employed by a monarch or chief. Concerning the former very little of a general nature can be said as there are local differences regarding the position they occupy. Among the Bambara for instance they belong to a separate group. Sometimes they are considered to be professional beggars, like the *gaulow* of Senegal.[5] Some are specialised in relating the history and genealogy of the tribe. They are expected to respect the truth. Others are concerned with inventing as much as possible and with telling everything in their own way.[6]

The narrator is powerful because he knows how to use words, but at the same time he is dependent on his fellow men. He is rich but also a beggar. He is feared by all because he can covertly ridicule a member of the audience or a well-known person during his performance. Through words he has close contact with the vital force, and by his rendering of mythical stories he touches on the deepest truths. He is the connecting link between god and man. Because of his exorcisms during ceremonies harmony is preserved in the community. The singer-poet plays an important part in all rites. He functions as coryphee and can at the same time be master of ceremonies, which does not mean that he necessarily has to perform the sacrifice or the magic himself. Often he acquires his texts by buying them, or otherwise he inherits them from his father. There are also feminine chanters in the women's rites.[7] In the ethnic grouping of Beti, Fang and Bulu the narrator is called *Mbôm-mvet,* which literally means 'he who strikes the zither'.[8] Socially he is highly regarded and enjoys many privileges.

> While he recites and sings, playing the zither, the *mbôm-mvet* is accompanied by an orchestra and a chorus. The orchestra is made up mainly of percussion instruments: little bells, rolled-up antelope hide, drums, iron rods or sticks beaten against each other. (The trunk of the banana tree, *nko'êkon,* sometimes replaces the antelope hide.) All those present form the choir, which is conducted by the wife of the *mbôm-mvet* or by someone else who knows the refrains and verses in the performing artist's repertoire.

> When the episode that he has told becomes dramatic the *mbôm-mvet* gives his zither to his wife, the whole orchestra continues playing and the choir keeps on singing, he mimes the play, possibly outlining some dance steps, and, with rising emotion, he begins to dance. Thus the dance, a more powerful means of expression, translates what cannot be expressed in words.[9]

Professional narrators are much scarcer than amateurs. Roland Colin[10] justly remarks that professionals do not have a monopoly on the magical word. In some societies there are no professional narrators at all. Male as well as female narrators exist. The well-known author Birago Diop[11] heard many of his stories from his grandmother, who used to tell them in the evenings till he fell asleep. Most narrators belong to the older generation. Stories are generally told in the evenings or at night, the reason being that 'it has always been the custom and that the parents and the grand-parents had done the same.' Certain subjects seem to be taboo during daytime. The tropical night becomes the background for a dramatic narrative, which can begin spontaneously in the family circle after the communal meal, or on special occasions when the whole village is gathered around the fire.

Normally the narrator accompanies himself on the zither, lute or harp-guitar, but he can also be accompanied by one or more musicians. He learns the art from a master who is called 'father', although it often is not his own father. It is not unusual for the 'father' to make him pay for his services, often in a symbolic manner.

When he begins the narrator refers to his 'sources'. For example:

> My father told me, and his father told him, and he heard it from someone else who bought it from another, who in his turn sold it . . .[12]

There are definite formulae for announcing the beginning and the end of a story, just as there is 'once upon a time . . .' Roland Colin[13] describes how, after the maize harvest, a special evening is organized among the Samos in West Africa. Maize cobs are grilled and the narrator sits among the listeners around the fire. At a given moment one of them asks one of the others, 'Have you seen my ring?' The answer is, 'I've given mine to X.' X then says, 'I've given mine to Z.' This type of talk goes around until someone says, 'I've given mine to so and so', at which stage he mentions the name of the narrator. He then pronounces the opening formula: 'Here comes my story . . . once upon a time . . .' It is possible that such a formula originally possessed a magical meaning and that the intention of it was to create the right atmosphere in which the myth could be revived.[14]

MYTHS AND EXPLANATORY STORIES

The terms myth, legend, saga, fairy tale and fable are more often than not confused or used carelessly, but these matters can hardly be discussed here.[15] Trying to delimit the field of the myth in Africa is exceedingly difficult. Bascom[16] notes that it is hardly possible to distinguish clearly between myth and legend in Africa, because no distinction is made between the sacred and the profane.

If the myth is intended to relate what has happened in the past and if it is always closely connected to religion and rite, if myths are supposed to contain the truth and if the dogmas and utterances in them are not to be doubted in the community, then Finnegan [17] is right in determining that the myth in this sense is not as prevalent in Africa as use of the term suggests.

> It is true that many of these so-called myths have an aetiological element, refer to supernatural beings, or are concerned with events set in some remote time in the past. But they do not necessarily also possess the other attributes of myth — their authoritative nature and the way in which they are accepted as serious and truthful accounts.

Finnegan's conclusion comes from what she had read and experienced. On the other hand it cannot be denied that faith in the truth of the myth was originally absolute and only later did it become corrupted and manipulated to a certain extent. It remains a fact that the boundary between myth and other, specifically explanatory stories, is very difficult to determine. With this reservation the term myth will be used here in future, but it has to be emphasised that the word should not be associated with the looser meaning of 'incredible fantasy' that it sometimes has in Western culture.

The myth serves also to embody abstract ideas regarding human existence. It is an ontology cast in the form of a story. In the myth there is an attempt to explain the origin of existence. One who does not know the myths of a people will not understand the most common rites of that people.[18] Man populates his world with gods and other supernatural beings and maintains that world by a system of rites. The ancestors are mediators between man and the gods. Ancestor worship is an important means of maintaining contact with the gods.[19]

Everywhere in Africa there are myths about the creation of the earth and the origin of the first man. Stories explaining how it comes about that things are as they are, are called aetiological stories. It goes without saying that as elsewhere in Africa answers have been sought to such questions as: How did it all begin? Where does death come from? Has it always been there? The Fulani of Mali tell a profound tale about creation and death that gives an indication of the hierarchy of forces that dominate the thoughts of their people:

> At the beginning there was a huge drop of milk.
> Then Doondari came and he created the stone.
> Then the stone created iron;
> And iron created fire;
> And fire created water;

And water created air.
Then Doondari descended the second time and he took
    the five elements
And he shaped them into man.
But man was proud.
Then Doondari created blindness and blindness defeated
    man.
But when blindness became too proud,
Doondari created sleep, and sleep defeated blindness;
But when sleep became too proud,
Doondari created worry, and worry defeated sleep;
But worry became too proud,
Doondari created death, and death defeated worry.
But when death became too proud,
Doondari descended for the third time,
And he came as Gueno, the eternal one,
And Gueno defeated death.[20]

Not only death, but the birth of children and animals
has always been a great mystery. The following story,
relating how death and children came into the world
and what the connection between them is, comes
from the Nupe of Nigeria.

God created the tortoise, men, and stones. Of each he
created male and female. He gave life to tortoises and
men, but not to the stones. None could have children,
and when they became old they did not die but became
young again.

The tortoise, however, wished to have children, and
he went to God. But God said: 'I have given you life, but
I have not given you permission to have children.'

But the tortoise came to God again to make his
request, and finally God said: 'You always come and ask
for children. Do you realise that when the living have

had several children they must die?'

But the tortoise said: 'Let me see my children and then die.' The God granted his wish. When man saw that the tortoise had children, he too wanted children. God warned man, as he had the tortoise, that he must die.

But man also said: 'Let me see my children and then die.'

That is how death and children came into the world. Only the stones did not want to have children, and so they never die.

An explanation is sought for creation, birth and death, while the origin and the invisibility of the various gods, natural phenomena, the physical characteristics of man and animal and much else pose questions: Why did God leave man?[21] Why are the sun and the moon in the sky?[22] Why are there good-looking and ugly people?[23] Where does fire come from?[24] Why is the sky so far away?[25] That sexes differ, that there are black and white people, that the bat does not fly during the day, that the wasp has such a thin waist and the tortoise carries a shield on its back: these are all explained in aetiological stories.[26] Traore[27] describes a performance he attended among the Fulani (Peul), a pastoral people in Senegal. It concerned the origin of the manatee, a kind of sea-cow. The people sat together next to the fire in the chief's enclosure. During the story the narrator plucked his guitar, stopping the music only for gestures or dancing with which to emphasise his words. The story about Penda who turns into a manatee, is very popular among these savannah dwellers.

Once upon a time there was a woman called Penda, the
most beautiful girl of the country Galam, a province of
Senegal. Her husband, Samba, was the best hunter the
country had ever known. On the day of Penda's marriage her mother gave her this advice: 'Be careful not to
appear naked before your husband!'

But it happened that Penda went swimming and that
her husband arrived at the moment when she was
getting out of the water. Shocked, Penda grabbed the
first object she could find to cover her nakedness.
This happened to be the winnower she was working
on before swimming. Covering her stomach with it
she dived into the water, begging the water spirit to
turn her into a fish so that she would not be shamed
before the people.

And the water spirit turned Penda into a large manatee
with breasts like a woman's. Until today this fish has at
the lower part of its body a patch that is nothing else
than the winnower Penda held to her stomach when she
dived into the water.

The story of Penda has clear aetiological characteristics. For the Fulani the manatee is a sacred animal.
The narrative ends with praise in its honour, a song
that the narrator and the audience sing together. The
metamorphosis of a woman into a fish, into a snake
or some water animal is very prevalent in African
myths. The seas and many rivers and lakes are in-
habited by water spirits and gods.[28] Soyinka uses
this theme in *The Swampdwellers*.[29] In the African
myth water can have the meaning of life force and
fertility. Some peoples bring offerings to the animals
which inhabit rivers in order to implore them for the

favour of the water gods or the ancestors. In this regard Holas[30] points out that the fish, snake, crocodile or tortoise is never to be confused with the authentic divine essence of which the animal is but a 'living image'.

THE ANCESTORS

Generally the first men spoken of in myths are also considered to be the first ancestors of a people. These and all later ancestors are considered to exert great influence on the living. Ancestors are worshipped as demi-gods and those who were tribal chiefs still have great power after death. They are consulted when important decisions are to be made, in judgements or at traditional ceremonies. It is necessary to respect them or they could punish the living by causing ill-nesses or accidents. They could cause rain to stop and pastures to dry out, harvests to fail or women to become barren.[31]

To obtain the favour of the forefathers, calm their anger or ensure their favourable disposition, sacrifices are offered to the dead. One example of a ritual text pronounced at such an occasion is given by Okot p'Bitek in *Horn of my love.*[32] He recorded the words from the original Acholi, a Ugandan language. One of the elders addresses the community, having received a message from the forefathers that a sacrifice must be brought to conciliate the dead. The text clearly shows that the whole community is involved in the event.

> Elder: The ancestors have spoken today;
>   Bring forth a brown billy goat,

Chicken and beer.
My father, you have asked for food;
Your food is here today;
Come to it now;
Call all your brothers,
Your food is here.

You my clansmen and clanswomen,
I have called you
Because of the food I have cooked for our
    fathers;
Come, let us give them food.
Today I hold a goat in my hand,
Let us give it to my father.

You, our fathers,
Accept the food we give you today;
Here is your food.
Why should we fear you?
You are our fathers.
You are our fathers.
Your billy goat is here,
Drink its blood today.
The fiends that are coming let them pass far
    away.
Your food is here today.
Let your children have good health;
Let the women have good childbirth,
So that your name may not be obliterated.
Your chicken is here;
Today we give you blood.
Let us have good health;
Let there be no deaths in the homestead.
If we were not here,
There would be no food for you.

Here, we give you beer;
Let us have good health,
Diseases that are coming,
Let them pass far away.

Today, I give you a goat;
Today, I give you blood;
Today, I give you beer;
I give you beer to quench your thirst.
Let us have good health.
Let there be silence, oh;
Let there be silence.

Today, we have cooked a feast for my father;
Today, I have given him food;
But, let there be silence.
Let the people have good health.

All:	Let the people have good health.
Elder:	Let the lions be killed.
All:	Let them be killed, killed, killed.
Elder:	Let our spears be sharp and straight.
All:	Let them be sharp, sharp, and straight.
Elder:	Let the women have good childbirth.
All:	Let them have good childbirth.
Elder:	Let the crops germinate well.
	Let the crops ripen well.
All:	Let the crops germinate and ripen well.
Elder:	Let the children's cries be heard.
All:	Let them be heard, heard, heard.
Elder:	The evil things that are in the homestead,
	Let the setting sun take them down in the west.
All:	Let it take, take, take.
Elder:	Let the setting sun take them.
All.	Let it take.

Elder: Let it take.
All: Let it take.
Elder: Let the setting sun take them.
All: And so it has taken them.

The bonds between the living and the dead cannot be broken. The patriarchs are the mediators between them because among the living they are the closest to eternity. There are no common traits which apply to all ancestors. Some have especially human, and at other times particularly divine characteristics attributed to them. The boundary between the two areas is difficult to determine. A forefather will try to help his offspring with the problems of life, but punish them when necessary. However it may be, the dead continue to live among the living. Birago Diop, the famous Senegalese narrator and poet, describes poetically in the story *Sarzan*[33] the different ways in which forefathers manifest themselves:

Listen more often
To Things than to Beings.
The Voice of the Fire is to be heard,
Hear the Voice of the Water.
Listen in the Wind
The Bushes are sobbing:
It's the breath of the ancestors.

Those who are dead have never left:
They're in the Shade that illuminates
And in the shade that becomes thick.
The Dead aren't under the Earth:
They're in the quivering Tree,
They're in the groaning Wood,
They're in the running Water,

They're in the standing Water,
They're in the Hut, they're in the Crowd.

Listen more often
To Things than to Beings.
The Voice of the Fire is to be heard,
Hear the Voice of the Water.
Listen in the Wind
The Bushes are sobbing:
It's the Breath of the dead Ancestors,
Who haven't parted
Who aren't under the Earth
Who aren't dead . . .

In the fragment from Okot p'Bitek as well as in the words of *Sarzan* there is much repetition of words, lines or whole stanzas.

The repetition of formulae, sentences, verses, songs and refrains which keep returning in the narrative typifies the oral character of this literature. Familiar words are enthusiastically recited or sung. More will be said about the way the song functions in the story.

THE EPIC

The heroic poem or epic is a well-known literary genre throughout the world. The epic has always been closely bound to history. In Africa the chronicle is known, recorded and passed on by a historian. The epic, on the other hand, is often a well-defined genre. But it also happens that in some societies no distinction is made between the two and that the one form merges with the other.

The historians in traditional communities have the

task of recording the genealogy of the chief, the migrations, battles, conquests, defeats and victories of the tribe. To the historian the actual events are important. For that reason he would be less concerned with artistic form than with an exact rendering of the facts. On the other hand the epic is more than a representation of historic events. The narrator of the epic wants to captivate his audience. As an artist he would subordinate the historical to the imaginative. There always remains a basis of truth from which the creative imagination of the poet functions. The epic is always concerned with one or more historical figures whose deeds live on in the memory of later generations. It is a characteristic of the epic that the main character, the hero of the story, really existed. Historical elements such as battles and conquests are authentic. However, in the epic the hero becomes more heroic and his deeds more miraculous than they were in reality. Miracles and magic are also found in the epic and gods and spirits sometimes play a role. The hero has become more than human. He is more than an ordinary ancestor and is often worshipped as a divinity.

These characteristics also apply to the epic poetry of Europe and Asia, where the epic is comparable to the African heroic poetry. Everywhere the epic is part of the oral tradition. Homer, a blind poet, recreated the Iliad and the Odyssey from traditionally handed-down records.[34] The *Song of Roland* and the cycle of William of Orange are examples from the ancient French epic, as is *Beowulf* from old English literature. They were narrated by troubadours, travelling singers and narrators, in the same way as epics are related in Africa.

Epics are long narrations, often cycles, which are

not suited to brief telling. The narration of an epic can last a whole night or several consecutive nights. Frobenius[35] has studied the epic literature of the Fulani. In Zaire among the Mongo the Lianja epic is often told[36] while among the Nyanga the Mwindo epic[37] is a favourite. The Mwindo epic was told in twelve days to Biebuyck and his associates by a bard from Kisimba, an isolated village in the province of Kivu. This man, She-Karisi Candi Rureke (She-Karisi means 'creator of an epic text'), narrated, sang and acted the many episodes of the Mwindo epic consecutively, but he told them that in reality it is not done in this manner. The whole epic is never told successively, but rather in a fragmentary fashion on different occasions.[38] Finnegan[39] says the same about similar epic narrative cycles.[40] The story of the Zulu hero Chaka was also passed down orally before being written down by Mofolo and translated into English by Dutton (1931). In recent years African epics have been transcribed more and more often and translated into European languages by researchers.

One of the best-known epics in African literature is *Soundjata,* which tells the story of the old Manding or Mali Empire. It was told in the Malinke language by an old narrator from the town of Djeliba Koro in the Siguiri (Guinea) area, and translated into French by Djibril Tamsir Niane. In his book Niane says that he merely looked at and listened to the old Manding narrators and that his story comes from them. 'I am only the translator, indebted to my masters,' he states in his preface.[41]

Soundjata is the hero of the story, which begins with the history of the first Manding kings. After that we are told about the parents of Soundjata, his illness and miraculous recovery. The battle against

Soumaoro Kante, the king of the Sosso, a neighbouring people, is an important episode. Soumaoro destroys the Manding empire and Soundjata, the
legendary king, becomes a ruler without a kingdom.
He receives support from people nearby and with
king Moussa Tounkara he goes out to encounter the
enemy in an attempt to reconquer his fatherland. The
decisive battle will be waged at Krina. Soundjata has
set up camp in the valley of the Djoliba.

Soundjata and Soumaoro had fought till then without
having declared war. One does not fight without saying
why. Warring parties ought to say in advance what they
have against one another. Just as the sorcerer should
bring evil to no one without laying blame, so the king
should not go to war without saying why he is taking up
arms. Soumaoro advances on Krina, close to the town
of Dayala on the river Djoliba, and decides to obtain
certainty before engaging in combat. Because Soumaoro
knew that Soundjata was also a sorcerer, he sent an owl,
entrusted with his words, instead of an envoy. The bird
of night alights on the roof of the tent of Djata and
speaks. In turn Soundjata, the son of Sogolon, also sends
an owl to Soumaoro. Here is the dialogue of the sorcerer kings:

Halt young man. Henceforth I am the king of Manding.
If you want peace return to where you come from.

I have returned, Soumaoro, to take back my empire. If
you want peace you will render your men harmless and
you will go back to Sosso, your own empire.

I am the king of Manding by force of arms. My right
has been established by conquest.

Then I shall take Manding from you by force of arms. I
shall drive you out of my kingdom.

Remember that I am the wild yam that grows on the

rocks. Nothing will drive me from the kingdom of Manding.

Do not forget that in my camp I have seven master-smiths who can blow up the rocks. And then, yam, I shall eat you.

I am the poisoned toad stool that can make the intrepid vomit.

I am the starved rooster. Poison does not affect me.

Be careful young man. You will burn your feet, I am the burning ash.

I am the rain that extinguishes the ashes. I am the rushing torrent that will carry you away.

I am the mighty kapok-tree that looks down from a great height onto the tops of other trees.

I am the stifling creeper that climbs to the top of the forest giant.

Stop the word-play. You will not get Manding back.

You know well enough that there is no place for two kings on one fleece, Soumaoro. Leave me your place.

You want war then, I shall wage war against you. Remember that I have killed nine kings and their heads decorate my room. Alas, your head will be placed near those of them who were as reckless as you are.

Prepare yourself, Soumaoro, for the evil that will strike you. Your men will not pass.[41]

The evening before the battle the singer and poet, Balla Fasséké, tells the soldiers the history of the Manding empire. Here we have something of a story within a story. The ancient history is recalled during a feast that Soundjata gives for his men. Balla Fasséké addresses himself in particular to Soundjata and explains to him that the time of which the spirits had spoken has arrived:

You, Maghan Soundjata, you are like the Manding empire. Both of you have known a long and difficult youth. Sixteen kings have been on the throne before you . . . sixteen generations have consolidated power. You hold the kingdom like the kapok-tree holds onto the ground with deep and mighty roots. To withstand the storm the tree needs long roots and gnarled branches. Maghan-Soundjata, has the tree not grown large? You are the son of Nare Maghan, but you are also the son of your mother, Sogolon, the buffalo-woman, before whom the sorcerers stagger in fear. You have the force and the majesty of the lion, you have the power of the buffalo.

I have told you what future generations will hear about your forefathers, but what will we tell our sons of you, that your memory will remain alive? What will our sons learn from our story? What unprecedented heroism, what unknown actions, what glittering weaponry will cause our sons to regret that they had not lived in the time of Soundjata? Poets are men of the word. Our words bring the deeds of kings to life, but the word is only the word. Power resides in action. Be a man of action. Do not answer me with the mouth. Show me tomorrow on the plain of Krina what you wish that I relate to coming generations. Make it possible for me to sing tomorrow the song of the vulture on the thousand corpses of Sossos cut down by your sabre before the evening.[43]

So on the eve of the great battle the history of the people is recalled. Soundjata and his men must show themselves in battle to be worthy descendants of their forefathers. Eventually, after a great battle and many losses, Soundjata and his men are victorious. He can return to his capital, Niani, as the victor. Thanks to the hero, Soundjata, peace reigns afterwards in

Manding and the country becomes very prosperous. Niani was considered the navel of the earth and everywhere in the furthest lands people spoke about this city, about Manding and Soundjata, even after his death and right up to today. The narrator ends the epic, telling about Soundjata's immortality. He also gives the names and surnames of his sources. It is necessary for the people to return home with the realisation of their insignificance as compared to these glorious ancestors.

> People of today, you are small compared to your ancestors, and limited in spirit, for you have hardly grasped the sense of my words. Soundjata now rests at Niani-Niani, but his spirit lives on, and even today the Keita (the princes) kneel at the stone under which the father of Manding rests. To acquire my knowledge I have travelled all over Manding. From great masters I have learnt how the kingdom originated. Everywhere I have seen and understood what my masters have taught me. In their hands I have sworn the oath to teach that which must be known and to be silent about that which must be concealed.

The Soundjata epic coincides mainly with the description by De Vries[44] of the lives of heroes according to Indo-Germanic sources. In the above fragments the musical aspect is not mentioned although it must have been an important element in the oral narration of the epic. The following stories will tell us more about the role of music.

STORY AND SONG

This is not the right place to discuss the various types
of music and song in Africa; eulogies, lullabies,
working songs, initiation songs, love songs, lament-
ations and religious songs.[45] We are concerned with
the way in which the song is functional in narratives
that do not have the element of worship.

Not every narration in Africa has a religious
background. There is a whole repertoire that is
without religious character and is not associated with
particular rituals or times of the year. The characters
are sometimes people and sometimes animals. The
stories are about miraculous events and beings,
about everyday people and things or about a
combination of both. There can be giants or monsters
in these stories, but sometimes they are quite realistic
renderings of relationships between brothers, friends,
men and women, parents and children; jealousy,
fidelity and infidelity, obedience, courage or
cleverness. In the Luba story about the giant
Tshilume-tshikulu (a story told to me by a Zairean
student), Tshilume is treated so badly by his petulant
and capricious wife that he leaves her. She then
suffers remorse for her bad temper and goes looking
for him. On the way she encounters the giant
Tshilume-Tshikulu. She is not afraid, but in her song
she questions him.

Tshilume-Tshikulu
large giant
have you not perhaps
seen my husband?
He is called Tshilume like you
and carries a whistle

on a string around his neck.

The giant pretends not to understand her and asks her to come closer. She moves closer, reaching his feet, and sings her song again. She has to climb onto his knee, then his hip, his shoulder, his beard and finally his lower lip. At every stage she repeats the song which the public repeats in chorus. After that she is swallowed by the giant and in his stomach she finds her husband and many others, a whole city. Thanks to the cleverness of the woman everyone is set free and the giant dies.

A similar story has been recorded in the Cameroons by Eno-Belinga among the Beti.[46] This is one of the many examples of stories that occur at quite different places in Africa while their structure and theme coincide greatly. Belinga, a musicologist, indicates meticulously where the story is told and where it is sung, and by whom, solo chorus. In the story *The girl and the Emômôtô* girls go swimming in a river. They leave in haste and the oldest forgets to take her belt. When later she returns to get it she meets the giant or Emômôtô who asks her what she has come to do. Up to that moment the story is told. Thereafter it is sung:

Solo:	I have come to fetch my belt
	that I forgot at the river.
Chorus:	Ayaya!
Solo:	I have come to fetch my belt
	that I forgot at the river.
Chorus:	Ayaya!
Solo:	It is the truth. I am not trying to evade.
Chorus:	I am not trying to evade. It is the truth.

Narration: The Emômôtô starts laughing. He says to the
          girl, 'I can't hear you so well. Come closer to
          my feet. Come closer.' The girl comes closer
          and speaks:

Song: I have come to fetch my belt
          that I forgot at the river.

This is repeated when the girl has to climb from the
foot to the knee, and after that still higher, finally to
be swallowed by Emômôtô. With the same cunning as
that of the wife of Tshilume in the Luba story, by
cutting open the stomach walls of the giant from the
inside and by sprinkling salt and hot pepper on the
wound, she frees herself and the other stomach
dwellers. In the Beti story they sing another song:

Solo: It's only a cut and nothing more.
Chorus: But it must have salt and hot pepper.

Solo and chorus repeat the song, alternating with
passages which tell how she executes her deadly
operation.

For the combination of music, song and story
Belinga introduced the term *Chantefable,* which
means 'an oral story or fable in which sung stanzas
are incorporated'. Text and melody form a
harmonious unity. The songs are an essential element
in the narration, not an accessory. Often the tune is
the 'motor' of the narration, the whole text resting
on the music.[47]

Because of the ability of soloist or choir to
improvise, songs are always being varied or expanded.
An example of this is the story of *Tawêloro* recorded
by Bernard Dadié.[48] Throughout the whole legend

the king repeatedly sings a song about Tawêloro, which means 'daughter of the woman'. The king and queen wait very long for the birth of a child and when Tawêloro is eventually born, they become so attached to the child that they deny her the right to marriage. In sorrow the girl leaves the house. From birth the queen has sung of the child's beauty:

My child is beautiful as the moon
    Tawêloro. Tawêloro.
My child is beautiful as the day
    Tawêloro. Tawêloro.

Tawêloro goes to the ocean. The waves, fish, crabs, plants, gulls, and sea urchins sing to her. With every new creature the refrain can be repeated, the whole of nature celebrating the departure of the princess.

The queen orders a search everywhere for her daughter. As soon as she realises that the child is lost she orders the drums beaten to send the message. The search seems fruitless and the mother, despite her advanced age, goes out herself. Everywhere she enquires about her daughter: from the Sun, the Day, the Night, the Wind, the Thunder, the Shade, the Rain, the Moon — and they all ask who Tawêloro is. As an answer the queen then sings a song in which she describes the beauty of her daughter.

My child is beautiful as the Moon,
    Tawêloro. Tawêloro.
My child is beautiful as the Sun,
    Tawêloro. Tawêloro.
My daughter is the ray of the lightning,
    Tawêloro. Tawêloro.
She is the delightful perfume of flowers,

Tawêloro. Tawêloro.
She is fresh as the dawn,
    Tawêloro. Tawêloro.
Supple as the waves,
    Tawêloro. Tawêloro.
Dazzling as the fire,
    Tawêloro. Tawêloro.
She is innocent as a new-born,
    Tawêloro. Tawêloro.
She is the smile of a child,
    Tawêloro. Tawêloro.
She is the hesitation of the moon,
    Tawêloro. Tawêloro.
Moon, have you seen my daughter?
    Tawêloro. Tawêloro.

When after years of travelling around the world the old mother finally arrives at the Moon and asks for Tawêloro, she notices that the Moon, also a mother, hesitates and does not reply immediately. The queen insists, singing loudly about her child. The Moon takes her to the ocean, and on the beach she addresses herself to the water, calling on everything again:

Sun, have you seen my daughter?
    Tawêloro. Tawêloro.
Day, have you seen my daughter?
    Tawêloro. Tawêloro.
Night, have you seen my daughter?
Ocean . . .

The ocean is silent and holds its breath. In the silence the queen hears the voice of her daughter, telling her that she will never return. She has become a mermaid.

Since that day the mother has been waiting on the beach for the return of her daughter. In the moonlight she can still be seen. 'She moves when you move and she's still when you are still, but she is always looking at the ocean and always singing.' Her song has become a lament.

My child is beautiful as the Moon,
   Tawêloro. Tawêloro.
My child is beautiful as the Day,
   Tawêloro. Tawêloro.
   Tawêloro o . . . o . . . o . . . o . . .

The theme of the woman who is actually a genie or naiad and sometimes lives for a while among humans occurs often in oral literature. In Zaire different peoples call her *mami wata*. In other places the mami wata has a threatening appearance. Holas[49] even speaks of 'the famous sea monster mami wata'.

In the oral literature there are many more songs than one would imagine, judging from published African stories. That these stories have not been recorded is probably because of the repetition of the songs, and because of the problems encountered in documenting and translating them. In reading the stories we do not ever get an exact impression of what happens during a public performance. This is not only true of the retelling of myths or the recitation of traditional poetry, but also of the telling of the epic, the fable and the farce. Finnegan[50] rightly says about the songs that they do not occur in every story and that in some areas a distinction is made between prose and choral narrations. Sometimes the song so dominates the performance that the story appears merely as a framework in which the songs can function. Much depends on the individual narrator, one attaching more importance to song than another will.

In the narration song is often used in the transition from one episode to another. An adventure might be ended with a song, the narrator being accompanied by the public. In the song the narrator is the soloist and the public the chorus.

THE ANIMAL WORLD AS A MIRROR OF THE HUMAN WORLD

The supernatural framework that stories often have makes it possible for the narrator not to be personally involved while criticising people in his audience. In this way he keeps a safe distance from the reality that he is attacking. For this reason people are often represented as animals. Everyone knows who or what is meant, but no one is directly put to shame.

There are clans that attribute a specific function to certain animals. An example has been given in the story of the manatee as it is told among the Fulani. Among the Bambara clan of the Diarra and the Wolof clan of the N'Diaye the lion holds a special position. Colin[51] remarks that this does not mean that the people would believe that this animal is really the mythical ancestor of the clan, but that

> a relationship exists between the position of the clan in
> the human family and the place of the lion in the
> animal family. This comparable position is explained as a
> similarity and is manifested in certain practices and rites.
> In this way the animals in the stories always fit into a
> (traditional, social) system.

Behind the animal mask and the animal character the human personality hides, with both good and bad qualities.

Little by little many African animal stories have been collected and translated. The central characters in the stories vary from one area to another. Often whole cycles are built around a few animals. The rabbit for instance appears almost everywhere that Bantu languages are spoken. In the forests of West and Central Africa the spider is the main character. The tortoise is found here as well, but also in Zambia. The small gazelle is the central character in a story cycle in North East Zaire and in Ruanda, while among the Luba in Kasai Kabundi the weasel excels in clever tricks. The mongoose plays a similar role among the Zulu and the Xhosa.[53]

Animals act as humans and the main characters solve problems by cunning and not by force. Often they save themselves in unexpected manner from painful situations or turn matters to their advantage at the cost of an opponent. Sometimes the main character is a greedy, boastful and stupid type and he eventually falls victim to his own bad characteristics. This is practically always the case with the hyena, and more often with the spider, Ananse. The stories are both instructive and amusing to the audience.

In a story told to me in Zaire and translated from Tshibindi the elephant is the clever one who solves problems with his great wisdom. Essentially the same story is told in *The Salary* which was recorded by Birago Diop in West Africa with the hare as the 'referee' and the crocodile as the thankless glutton.[54] The latter role is played in the Tshibindi story by the hyena, who is always treated unsympathetically.

Close to the village of Katwala Bashi Kashiwoe there once lived a hyena who spent all his nights searching for prey. One night he fell into a well. The well was so deep that his attempts to get out were unsuccessful. The next morning he was still in the well, calling for help. A fat ox, hearing him, peeped over the edge and saw the hyena.

— Is that you, ox?

— Yes it's me.

— Uncle ox, the hyena called with his sweetest voice. Please help me out of this well. Let your tail hang down, then I'll hold onto it so that I can get out.

— You're bad, said the ox. Everyone knows that. You're the one who devoured the two month-old heifers.

— That's a lie, said the hyena. When it's dark people confuse me with others.

— I know that you're a bad beast, the ox repeated. If I help you out of that hole, then you'll try eating me as well.

— Please, uncle ox, the hyena begged. I swear I'll be your best friend, if you help me out of the well.

The ox, a friendly animal, let his tail hang down into the hole. The hyena clung to it and in this manner he was pulled out. Alas! He was hardly saved when he fell upon the ox and started biting him. Luckily for the ox the elephant was just passing by. — What is happening here? Aren't you ashamed of attacking each other like children? Please be calm. Come here both of you then I'll discuss matters with you as we do in our part of the bush. The ox almost died. He was wounded so badly that he could not say a word, while the hyena told one lie after the other. — It seems a complicated history to me, said the elephant. I suggest that both of you go back to the start. I have to see how the fight started, so that I can understand what happened. The hyena who

was as stupid as he was wicked, jumped back into the well.
— I see, said the elephant. Well, that's that. Now you can each do as you like.
To the ox it seemed wise not to listen to the hyena a second time. The hyena remained in the well, and it is told that he is still there.

PUPPET SHOWS AND MASQUERADES

Labouret and Moussa Travéle[55] describe forms of puppet shows found among the Somono in Niger and in various Hausa towns. Other forms seem to exist in the Republic of Benin, in Nigeria, as well as among the Basanga, the Tshokwe and the Luba of Zaire.[56] Finnegan mentions other places where the puppet show is also found: in the north of the Ivory coast, in Bornu, Zaria, Bida and some places in Northern Nigeria and Niger, and also locally in the south of Nigeria.[57] She mentions a description by Ellison[58] who was a spectator at a puppet show in Bornoe, in which dolls made of cloth that fitted the hand of the player like a glove, performed in the entrance to a kind of tent. The tent consisted of a wide sheet of cloth draped around a pole. Eight different sketches are performed, each three to four minutes long. There are never more than two puppets on the 'stage' at the same time and as many as six different puppets play one part. Between the acts singers and drummers perform for the public. The scenes are complete in themselves and each has its own dialogue, matching costumes and a dramatic line of action. The chief preoccupation here is again who beats and who is beaten, as is always the case with the oldest form of drama. 'The origin of all drama is invariably a fight.'[59]

The popular West African masquerades are dances of costumed figures wearing masks. The masquerades vary from one area to another, but they all have elements of the theatre. The players depict spirits or ancestors, sometimes also clownish figures and women. Music and dancing are a necessary part of the performance, while the verbal element plays a subordinate role, although 'there is sometimes a rudimentary plot'.[60]

There is always some kind of religious element. It is believed that the masked figures are somehow supernatural or connected in some manner to supernatural beings. Women and the initiates have profound respect for the masked ones. As with the Gelede masquerades,[61] the religious aspect seems to have become subservient to the aesthetic in some cases. Fear is less important while jokes and comical elements are more prominent. The 'spiritual plays' of the Ibo and the Ibibio are played by actors representing definite types, male and female, with the aid of masks (feminine roles are also played by men). Pantomime, parody and satire is found here, while commentaries and songs accompany the play.[62] In the masquerades the verbal element never predominates. It is 'the language of the dance' that makes the events so attractive to the public. In general in the masquerades language is subservient to music, song and especially dancing.[63]

Among the Yoruba there are also masquerades, such as those of the Egungun society, a group that guards the spirits of the ancestors. When a particular ancestor is chosen to be honoured a mask is carved for him. There are also masks in which participants depict animals.[64] A specific drum rhythm will be part of a particular masquerade. The dancers wearing the masks adapt their voices to identify themselves with the figure they are representing. The Egungun masks are (out of respect?) seldom called by the name of the ancestor to which they are consecrated. The masks are tangible means for making contact with the supernatural. When the dancer goes into a trance it is believed that the spirit of the forefather has taken possession of him and that he is dominated by the will of the spirit whose mask he is wearing.

The poetry accompanying the dance is not only expressed in words, but more often by the rhythm of the drum. The message formulated through the drum rhythm supplies the necessary instructions to the dancers and clarifies the theme of the ritual.[65] A modern playwright like Wole Soyinka makes use of masquerades in various plays, such as *The Road*.[66] J.P. Clark based his play *Ozidi*[67] on an Ijaw myth told during masquerade plays and expressed in music, mime and dance.

SHORT COMEDIES AND FARCES

In many of the dramatic forms so far discussed the various principal roles are played by the same actor. That is not the case with the masquerades where, as we have seen, the text is often less important. Neither is it the case in the shorter plays where village life is expressed by different actors, each representing a type in a way that is strangely reminiscent of the *commedia dell'arte*. Often hunters, warriors or farmers play the lead. The most popular themes are the jealous husband being ridiculed, the frivolous woman, the braggart, the lover caught by surprise, the villain or the glutton. Nowhere is there a detailed description of these *sayètes,* as they are called in French. Alphamoye Sonfo[68] describes two in an article about African theatre. He has taken his information from the well-known anthropologist Delafosse, who recorded these farces among the Bambara in 1916. They are comic plays that attempt to amuse and instruct the public. They end happily, the problems are eventually solved, the battle-axe is buried, evil punished and virtue rewarded.

The success of plays like the one following depends entirely on the acting and the improvising talent of the actors.

The wife, husband and her lover.

The play is acted on the village square. The spectators and the musicians sit in a circle.

A man and a woman enter and introduce themselves to the members of the orchestra as if they are strangers. The orchestra represents the notables of the village. The players ask permission to live in the village and are accepted. With his foot the man draws an outline on the ground to represent the house that he has built. In the meantime the woman walks around on the 'stage' close to the audience. She sees a man (the actor) whom she would like to have as a lover, but because there is no chance to realize her idea nothing happens. With a stick her husband scratches the ground, representing the cultivation of his land. He sows and awaits the harvest. The reaping of the crop is also enacted. Together the man and the woman cut the *da* (a kind of sorrel) and lay it on a heap. Its seed is used in the kitchen. The woman makes use of the opportunity to meet her lover. She says something like, 'The *da* is dry. I'm going to grain it'. The man agrees.

The woman runs off to her lover and makes an appointment with him for the following morning. She can hardly control her excitement and her joy and it is not long before her husband becomes suspicious. The next morning the lovers meet in the field. The husband appears on the other side of the 'stage' with a basket and a pick. He acts as if he is busy breaking up pieces of termite mound for his chickens. The woman sees him and quickly hides her lover under the heap of *da* plants. Her husband who has seen everything comes and sits down comfortably with her, takes a pinch of snuff and says calmly to his wife, 'Have you finished graining the *da*?'

Woman:	Yes, I've finished. The grains are in the basket.
Husband:	Good. You take the *da* grains home then I'll soon bring the ash.
Woman:	(Nervous) What ash?
Husband:	Oh, I'm going to burn this mountain of old *da* plants.
Woman:	(More nervous) Burn it tomorrow. Let's go home now.
Husband:	(Firm) No. I'm not in a hurry to go home. I'm going to burn it now.
Woman:	(Irritated) Don't you see the clouds. Don't you feel the wind?
Husband:	(Acting stupid) Yes, yes, I see, but when it rains I'll cover the ash with my clothes.
Woman:	The wind will carry everything away.
Husband:	(His voice becoming authoritarian) I'm not going home before I've burnt all the *da* plants.

(He starts making a fire and lighting the plants. Then the woman takes a shawl and starts dancing around the *da* mountain, singing).

Woman: Long *da* plant, Koulibali, forgive me! The master of the *da* says that he won't go from here without the ash of his *da* plants. (She repeats the song several times).

When the plants start burning the lover comes out and starts running. The husband runs after him, calling out, 'Catch the rat who escaped from under my *da*!' This call is repeated several times. The public laughs, the wife disappears and eventually the two men leave the scene running.

Finnegan[70] describes the West African comic performances, which she gets from Labouret and Travélé.[71] These concern satirical pieces known as *kote kome nyaga*, plays about the vagaries of marriage or other aspects of life. The authors of plays also perform in them. Early in the evening it is announced that the *kote koma nyaga* will begin. The people hurry to the open village square, while the children play among the spectators. The drum orchestra sits in the middle and the young men and women begin dancing in a circle to a slow rhythm. After that the orchestra withdraws to a corner of the square, with the encircling chorus of women and girls supporting the song of the players.

In the meantime the players (men almost always play the female roles as well as the male ones) prepare themselves in a nearby house. They cover their faces and bodies with clay or ash to look strange or comical and they wear matching clothes. When the players are ready they are announced and there is silence. An invisible actor addresses the audience in terms that are familiar to them. He is answered line for line by the choir. Then the actor hesitantly makes his entry, his half-naked body covered in ash. He wears an old turban on his head and is dressed in rags. The orchestra encourages him to call the others. This he does in a comic manner with exaggerated impatience while running from one entrance to the other and listening to hear if they are not yet arriving. When the other players eventually appear everyone is costumed to fit his role: a decrepit old man, a blind man, a cripple, a leper, an idiot, a clumsy hunter, a villain, an adulterer, a deceived husband, a thief and a murderer. They go round the circle formed by the audience singing and dancing. When they retire the prologue has ended.

After this the comedies follow one another with themes like 'The bragging coward', 'The unfaithful wife', 'The cheated hunter', 'The magician with the big ears' and 'The yam thieves'. These plays from the former French Sudan (the ancient empire of Mali) closely resemble the play Delafosse recorded among the Bambara. They also use the term *kote koma nyaga* for it.

Often the researcher is warned against the assimilation of ritual and theatre. As Alain Ricard[72] points out in his *Théâtre et nationalisme,* it is extremely difficult to distinguish between ritual ceremony and theatrical ceremony, between lived theatre and enacted theatre, between participation and performance.

In modern theatre the African playwright uses

traditional devices for his own purposes.

> When reinterpreted the ritual is betrayed, but such
> betrayal confers a new value. The ritual belongs to an
> archaic society in which kinship forms one of the
> essential networks. Social differentiation is not pro-
> moted therein. Modern African theatre wants to be part
> of the theatre of modern states, with universal found-
> ations, where differentiation of the parts increases
> with industrialisation and urbanisation. It is normal that
> the writer becomes more individualistic, the actors
> become more specialised and that the audience gets
> organised. But this does not necessarily mean the
> extinction of traditional culture.[73]

Such 'creative betrayal' (the expression is Robert
Escarpit's) will be the subject of the following
chapter.

FOOTNOTES-

1. cf Burns 1973, p 23.
2. 1972, p 2.
3. cf Lord, 1960, cf. Finnegan, 1970.
4. 1965, p 112.
5. Eno-Belinga 1965, p 115.
6. cf Menga, 1974.
7. Alexandre and Binet 1958, quoted by Eno-Belinga.
8. Bebey 1969, pp 42 ff, Towo-Antangana, 1966, pp 8 ff.
9. Eno-Belinga 1965, p124.
10. 1965, p 145.
11. 1962, 1963, 1965.

12. Eno-Belinga 1965, p 116.
13. Roland Colin 1957, p 84.
14. Finnegan 1970, pp 380, 381.
15. cf Lüthi 1970, 1974, cf Shipley 1970.
16. 1965, p 481.
17. 1970, p 362.
18. Dieterlen 1951, p XIX.
19. Holas, 1968.
20. Beier 1979, pp 1, 2.
21. Mende, Sierra Leone; Dinka, Sudan.
22. Fanti, Ghana.
23. Yoruba, Nigeria.
24. Ila, Zambia; Pigmies, Zaire; Dogon, Mali.
25. Bini, Nigeria.
26. Basset 1883, Beier 1974, Carey 1970, Knappert 1971, Parrinder, 1973.
27. 1958, pp 33, 34.
28. Parrinder, 1973, 83ff.
29. 1969, cf also Ogunyemi, 1973.
30. 1968, p 194.
31. Holas 1968, 122 ff.
32. 1974, pp 93 – 95.
33. 1965, pp 180 – 183.
34. Lord 1960.
35. Finnegan 1970.
36. Boelars 1957, 1958, De Rop 1964.
37. Biebuyck 1965, 1978.
38. Biebuyck 1971, p 274.
39. 1970 p 370, 371.
40. cf Knappert (1958) who studied the Swahili epic of Heraklios in East Africa.
41. Niane 1961, p 9.
42. Ibid, pp 112 – 114.
43. Ibid, pp 116 – 118.
44. 1959.

45. Finnegan 1970, Beier 1971, Kesteloot 1967, pp 338 — 340.
46. Kesteloot 1967, pp 338 — 340.
47. Eno-Belinga 1965, pp 55 — 56.
48. 1966, pp 77 — 81.
49. 1968, p 195.
50. 1970, pp 385, 386.
51. 1965, p 91.
52. Colin 1965, p 92.
53. Finnegan 1970, p 344.
54. 1965, pp 99 — 105.
55. 1928.
56. Labouret and Travélé 1928, p 24, Beier 1973, pp 224 — 245.
57. 1970, pp 503, 504.
58. 1935.
59. Van der Leeuw 1955, pp 96, 97.
60. Finnegan 1970, p 509.
61. Beier 1973, p 243.
62. Jones 1945.
63. Horton 1963, 97 ff.
64. Rotimi 1971, 43 ff.
65. Laurence 1969, 13 ff.
66. 1971.
67. 1961.
68. 1971.
69. Sonfo 1971, pp 75, 76.
70. Finnegan 1970, 505 ff.
71. 1928.
72. 1972, p 59 ff.
73. Ibid, p 61.

III. The Oral Tradition:
a Source of Inspiration

However diverse the oldest forms of theatre in Africa may be, they almost always are concerned with the need of man to ensure his existence in the midst of dangers. This need, in fact, exists always and everywhere. Even western man has a need for security and modern theatre also attempts to hold a mirror to people in which they can examine their world.

In traditional society the religious system determines the cultural unity of the people. Life forces bind man to his past, his present and his future and determine his relations with gods, spirits, nature and natural phenomena. This unity tends to break down where western influence increases. Certain political, social and economic organisations may change drastically, and even linguistic and cultural forms may be altered. Traditional theatre confirms the existing order and keeps the community together. It is popular theatre intended for and appreciated by all. However, the increasing influence from outside has not left African theatre unaffected.

THE 'WILLIAM PONTY SCHOOL'

At school and at university African students come into contact with Shakespeare, Molière and Racine. Missionaries introduced Christmas and Easter plays, mysteries and moralities which were prepared and performed with talent and enthusiasm during church festivals. At the same time the clergy opposed the African rituals and tried to have them abolished. This had the effect that for some time Africans looked down upon their own culture and lost interest in it. However, some colonisers did try to promote African culture. One example is the William Ponty school in Senegal, where subaltern cadres were trained for the French colonial administration of West Africa.[1] In the thirties, the director, Carles Béart, asked students to investigate their own oral tradition. Based on recorded stories and traditions 'indigenous' plays were then performed in French during festive occasions to an audience of students, teachers and the local African bourgeoisie. Such evenings were very successful, but the measure of colonial control and paternalism should not be underestimated.

The intention was always to assimilate students into the colonial system. Many of these students had a more critical approach towards their own customs than towards western norms.

Certain West African French writers of the first generation went through the William Ponty school, were influenced by it, and eventually criticised the way in which instruction and cultural training were given. Some of them like Bernard Dadié,[2] Boubou Hama[3] and Fily Dabo Sissoko,[4] wrote about it in their autobiographical works. After the fifties the theatrical activities of the William Ponty school had almost disappeared because the structure of the school had changed and the programme left little time for leisure.

Until then the school had yielded to the wishes of the colonial administration. Cultural instruction had excluded discussion of the colonial system, the intention being to keep the minds of the young away from contemporary politics. In most cases this succeeded. Traore searched for the use of historical sources in the William Ponty theatre and came to the conclusion that there was no trace of African nationalism to be found in it. On the contrary the writers of the William Ponty school

> presented the old African monarchs no different than the official colonial history did, i.e. as bloodthirsty tyrants.[5]

There was also a strong French influence in the form of the plays. Presentations took place in a closed, covered area and on a stage with décor, while the curtain underlined the clear distinction between players and audience. The verbal element (and the French language) were dominant. Entrance money had to be paid, so that the audience remained limited to a small elite, symptomatic of the new structures beginning to develop in the colonial society.[6]

THE NIGERIAN FOLK OPERA

By the amalgamation of European and African elements in English West Africa the Nigerian popular opera was born, of which Rotimi[7] gives the following definition: '(It) covers that type of presentation that thrives on music, song, dance, extended story-line, a message of a moral nature which is sometimes made obvious in the title of the play, broad acting gestures, and the vernacular of the people which may range from an isolated local dialect to commonly understood pidgin English.' The themes often come from mythology or other traditional narratives, and for performances the songs are rehearsed and the dialogue improvised. This popular genre developed only during the twenties and the thirties in the independent African churches, such as the Apostolics and the Seraphim and Cherubim group. The biblical stories and moralities that these church groups enacted and which were undoubtedly introduced by the missions soon made way for secular plays in which an important place was given to social and political satire. They are still performed by itinerant groups that have been in existence since the beginning of the forties.[8]

A simple stage is used so that it can be erected quickly. The dialogue is presented in lively Yoruba. The costumes are colourful and the acting is supported by impressive drum and choral rhythms. One example is the adaptation to folk opera of Tutuola's *Palm Wine Drinkard*.[9] This is performed everywhere in Nigeria, and beyond its borders (at the Pan African Festival in Algeria in 1969 for example). In this connection Bakary Traore writes,

Nigeria has given us (i.e. French speaking Africa) a lesson in authenticity, as much by the use of the language, the Yoruba (the audience does not have to know the language to understand the beautiful mimes, dances and songs), as by the proficiency of the actors, the mixing of genres, dance, song and symbols. The author-actor (ogunmola) is an accomplished artist.[10]

Here one finds something of a difference in colonial cultural politics. The French, at least in West Africa, were more paternalistic and more concerned with assimilation than the English who considered cultural differences as politically irrelevant. The French assimilation policies have caused reactions throughout the years, the negritude movement being one of the consequences.[11]

Probably because of this, French speaking Africans have felt the need to theorize about authenticity, and have only recently via this detour reached their 'sources'.

According to Rotimi[12] the essential link which binds the traditional drama with the Yoruba folk opera and later with the Nigerian theatre in English, is the inevitable moralization. The folk opera includes a lot of dancing and singing, but there is also a story.

Duro Ladipo was the first Yoruba writer-director who thought that a well-produced text was important. He was both musician and author. Ladipo's plays have a strong traditional basis. He studied different song and dance techniques from Yoruba culture and he made use of *oriki* (praise names), *ijala* (hunting songs) and *iwi* (masquerade poetry) in plays such as *Oba Koso* and *Oba Waja*.[13]

He also influenced other Nigerian writers like Obotunde Ijimere.[14] Today the tradition is continued through the folk opera. Ogunyemi calls his work *Obalúayé*[15] a music-drama, but, according to the introduction, this does not mean that music and drama are the only elements. Music, dancing, drama, décor and light effects unite towards a multi-faceted performance, which he calls 'five dimensional'.

The comprehensive materials making up the African theatre cannot be divided into tragedy, comedy or bourgeois drama.

MYTHS AND ANCESTORS

The oral tradition is clearly dominant in *The Exodus* by the Ugandan writer Tom Omara.[16]   This is a historical story from the present-day land of the Acholi, east of the Nile, in northern Uganda. Essentially it is an aetiological story with a mythical character in which an explanation is given for the fact that two related clans do not live on the same side of the river. In Omara's version the play is introduced by a narrator who has collected a group of children around him. They sit in front of the stage or among the audience, and with questions and answers the attention of the audience eventually moves to the stage and the real actors. According to the author a narrator could summarise this first part as follows:

> Long, long ago, before anyone was born, God, the Moulder, the Nameless One, lowered to earth the First Man. Lwo was his name. Then the world was bare, like an egg's surface. There was nothing like buildings, cars, clothes, or even people, except for this single man, Lwo. So that from Lwo spring all the people now alive, you and me. Lwo had a grand-daughter who bore forth triplets. These brothers lived a life that was cursed by quarrels and jealousies. One day there was such a big quarrel that they split up, and for ever after lived on opposite sides of the great river.[17]

If one of the children proposes to enact the story, the

narrator remarks that the song must first be sung, which according to tradition has to precede such a 'revelation'. They sing the Acholi song *Canna*, after which the play is performed 'on stage'. The narrator does not perform again. The language of this short play is solemn, the dialogues written in free verse. There is hardly any music, no singing (except at the beginning) and no dancing. It ends with a ceremony in which the brothers swear on their crossed spears that they will separate forever. *The Exodus* was a great success in East Africa, but it had a cool reception in England, perhaps because of the verse and because of the tradition that the material's source remains unknown. The play is still very close to the narration that must have been handed down originally.

The situation is different with the plays of John Pepper Clark, in which many European and American readers and playgoers have 'discovered' influences of Greek drama. This is because of the often solemn verses (as in the work of Omara), the role of the choir, themes of kinship, the curse on a family, incest, the presence of a prophet or a prophetess, the revenge of the gods and so forth. Clark denies that his sources are primarily Greek, but it must be allowed that similarities could have existed between the society of the Greeks during the time of Sophocles or Euripides and the traditional Ijaw society from which this writer comes.

In his first play, *Song of a Goat*[18] he makes use of Ijaw mythology and tradition to a much larger extent than in *Ozidi*.[19] The Ijaw fishing villages are situated in the mangrove swamps of the Niger delta, where the daily life of the inhabitants is ruled by the presence of the forefathers, water-spirits and water-gods who inhabit the creeks and marshes. Ijaw masquerade players of the Ekine community perform a cycle each year consisting of thirty to fifty plays which begin with a procession to the sacred river bank where the water spirits are called up and taken to the town. At the end of the cycle all masquerade players perform together before they finally go to the beach and the spirits are sent from the masks back to the creeks.

Unlike the Greeks (Oedipus for instance) the Ijaw do not regard the fate of man as inevitable. Destiny can be influenced, not by the individual, but by the observation of the appropriate rites.[20]

During the masquerade plays the Ozidi story is told over seven days and depicted with the aid of song, dance and mime. Clark has also filmed the whole event and recorded it on tape. His own play is divided into five acts, beginning with the scene in which the water spirits are called up. While the audience is being seated the narrator comes up, claps his hands and demands attention, because before the play a sacrifice must be made. For this seven virgins from the audience are needed. These girls have to 'build a bridge between those present and the guests from the sea'. The girls each receive a plate filled with offerings and follow the man. They are followed by the orchestra, chorus, actors and dancers, and in procession they sing a solemn song. When the narrator invokes the water-spirits everyone is silent. The formula is reminiscent of the Acholi sacrificial ritual which was described earlier, but the text has been adapted to suit changing times, as is always the case with the oral tradition. When the offerings have been made, the narrator says, among other things:

> And now that you have taken of
> Our food and of our drinks,
> Please give us good wives.
> Give us good children, and give us good money, too.
> After all, in Lagos, Benin, Ibadan, Enugu and
> Kaduna we hear people are now running into streams of
>   riches right up to
> Their necks. Men that yesterday were only teachers,
> Depending on schoolboy collections and firewood,
> Or shoemakers peeling their own soles to eat
> Are today ministers of state riding in cars as big as
>   ships.[21]

After the ceremony the whole group sits in a half-circle and the palm wine is sent around. The group now forms the council meeting of the city or Orua, where the narrator plays the role of Ozidi. The elders discuss the succession to the throne. During recent years all ruling kings of Orua died in quick succession. They want to have Ozidi as king. His house is the next in line of succession, but because he is the youngest and because his elder brother Temugedege is mad, he refuses on behalf of both. Then suddenly his brother appears with the news that he wants to become king. Although everyone believes that it cannot be, no one opposes him. The coronation takes place, after which the insane king is inviolable; a situation that Ozidi expressly wanted to prevent. When he criticises his brother he is ambushed and killed by the elders. His young wife Orea gives birth to their only son after his death. He is also called Ozidi and becomes a great fighter like his father. His strength can partially be attributed to his grandmother Oreame who has mystical powers and has decided to avenge the death of her son-in-law. Ozidi

takes back the kingdom, but has no peace. He is
always filled with the urge to go into battle. His
grandmother encourages him and protects him at
critical moments, binding him to her. Eventually he
kills her (intentionally or not, we are not told) while
blinded by the magic herbs with which she touched
his eyes. The last act is played alternately in the
house of Orea, where Ozidi is ill with 'pocks', and on
the river bank where all kinds of allegorical figures
like the King of Pocks, Cough and Fever appear.
Before the healing of Ozidi his mother has to perform
a purification ritual, which she does by calling up the
god, Tamara. In this manner she forces the King of
Pocks and his followers to leave the country and the
house of Ozidi. When the procession returns the
narrator, in his role as Ozidi, leads a train of all the
actors in a final dance, 'in which the audience may
take part'.[22]

Not only its theme and masquerade form relates
Ozidi to African society: the language also relates to
the Ijaw society in which the play is performed. To
westerners the language may sometimes seem
rhetorical, but this is the language of West Africa, full
of comparisons, riddles, idioms, images from tradition,
from nature and daily life.[23] When the elders of the
village have come to the decision that the young
Ozidi also has to be killed, one says of him,

> This is no time to wail like women
> Who have lost their wares at market. We must
> Start work at once. Ewiri, we greet
> You for bringing us this warning.
> Azezabife, Oguaran,
> Agbogidi, up with arms and whatever
> To hand, but only in our self defence.

Remember that. If first we look for a stick
Long enough, we shall never kill the snake
In the house. So rise,
Rise, I say rise at once.[24]

Names also play a role, as can be seen at the beginning, during the meeting about the succession, where
Ozidi rhetorically asks the praise-name of each. Such
names are not always praise names. Often they
merely refer to specific characteristics or physical
features.[25] In this way Ozidi greets and is greeted by
Azezabife, the 'Skeleton Man', and Oguaram, or the
'Man of twenty toes and twenty fingers'.

Much more can be said about Clark's work than is
possible here. Sometimes he does not know enough
about the technical possibilities of the theatre. For
that reason there is often too much happening behind
the scenes and the symbolism in the play is not
always transmitted to the reader. His language,
however, is poetical and in his search for the role
of fate in human life he touches on universal
problems.

HISTORY AND EPIC

It is impossible to make an exact distinction in oral
literature between myth, history and epic. This is
even more so with the plays derived from these
'genres'. Much depends on the interpretation that a
writer gives to his source. In *Abraha Pokou, ou Une
grande africaine*[26] Charles Nokan (Ivory Coast) draws
the line from myth and ancestors via history through
to the topical. The story of this queen is told in
written history.[27] It goes back to the oldest history

of the Baule from the Ivory Coast, a suppressed
people leaving their territory to live elsewhere in
freedom. Followed by the hostile Ashanti they come
to a river, and to prevent a massacre the queen
Pokou sacrifices her young child to the water gods,
who then make the crossing possible. A kapok
tree bends over from the other side and the people
climb across. The tree straightens itself before the
enemy reaches the bank. The queen is the last to
reach the opposite side, where the people kneel down
before her. She can only say *'Baouli'*, which means
'the child is dead'. Since then the people have taken
the name Baule.

Pokou not only sacrifices everything for her
people, but she also represents the ideal of the future
of Africa where exploitation and oppression will be
eliminated, where slaves will not exist anymore and
where women will have the same rights as men. In
Pokou's new empire there are enemies, but they are
conquered. In the introduction Nokan cites Mao Tse
Tung, and he dedicated the play to the women
of Africa, who must be 'like their sisters from Viet-
nam'. According to Nokan

> The African artist must fight against cultural imperial-
> ism, colonialism and neo-colonialism and their black
> agents. He has to protect national culture, enrich it,
> make it revolutionary and consecrate his work to the
> battle for a better life for all the suppressed . . .[28]

The epilogue of *Abraha Pokou* is characterised by the
same style. It is spoken by the 'Poet of Today'
together with spectators, a kind of credo for the
Revolution.

Nokan is one of the many African writers who tries

to change society by means of his work, but his slogan-filled language does not suit the Baule whom he uses to preach his gospel.[29]

Pas de feu pour les antilopes by the Zaireans, Mushiete and Mikanze, has educational intentions, but here message, language and tradition are better unified. It was first performed in Kinshasa in 1969 as part of a national campaign for the protection of nature.

It has long been the custom in Africa to burn parts of the savannah and bush in the dry season so that the animals are frightened and the hunt is made easy. This is what happens in Kipwala, home of the greedy chieftain, Manga. In the dry season he is always destroying large expanses of bush and savannah to make his hunting easy. The area becomes impoverished and the inhabitants starve. Many people leave the town permanently. One of them is Mayama, who settles in the neighbouring town of Benga, where the active and sensible chieftain Mukoko rules. Mayama learns that it is possible to do things differently, and armed with this knowledge he returns to his own village. But chief Manga will not heed his good advice. Mayama is imprisoned and Manga declares war on Mukoko and his village. When the two groups of fighters are face to face, the old and peace-loving bard Kapaya makes a suggestion.

Brothers of Kipwala and Benga. The ancients say, 'The wise puts the fool in his proper place'. We shall see that today. When our forefathers settled in these areas, they decided to live as good neighbours, as friends, and they instructed us to continue that tradition. They forbade us to make war on each other, but because of what we have experienced Manga, the chieftain of Kipwala, has

challenged Mukoko, the chieftain of Benga, and given
him the choice of weapons. Well, Mukoko suggests
that both chiefs test their strength by dancing![30]

While the drums beat and the people sing en-
couragement to the chiefs, Mukoko and Manga dance,
at first in slow rhythm, then gradually quicker and
quicker, until Manga falls into the dust. The people of
Benga cheer and Mukoko, the victor, orders his
opponent to sail away in a canoe and to find a new
home somewhere else. Mayama is taken out of prison
and chosen as headman of Kipwala. Both villages have
a feast. The central characters are soberly sketched in
contrast to plays where the hero is taken from
history. From the example of the Soundjata epic we
have already seen how dramatic historical events can
be recreated to afford the hero the opportunity of
saving himself by using his exceptional wisdom
and wonderful strength.

History is also used to teach people something
about the present. In his play *Tanimoune*[31] André
Salifou of Niger presents the history of Damagaram, a
fertile kingdom from Central Sudan in the nineteenth
century, of which Tanimoune was the most
important king. In the introduction Salifou says that
his most important aim is to show his countrymen
'one of the greatest figures from pre-colonial Niger'.
He respects the true facts, but wants at the same time

> . . . to make known the wise voice of the ancestors to
> the fanciful 'negro kings' of the twentieth century.
> Fundamental matters such as the rights and the freedom
> of a people will be questioned here, just as the problem
> of authority that even now the great of the earth do not
> always obtain legally, and which they misuse.[32]

It is striking how many playwrights use historical heroes in their work. Eugène Dervain (Ivory Coast), for example, devotes two plays to Da Monzon, a hero from the Bambara tradition.[33] Cheik Ndao sketches the noble characteristics of Alboury N'Diaye in *L'exil d'Alboury*.[34] According to the writer 'reality and imagination' merge in this play. Apart from Alboury and a few others, the characters are fictional.

> What does it matter? A historical piece is not a historical thesis. It is my intention *to create myths that can give new life to the people and help them forward.*[35]

In Ndao, which received the first prize at the Pan African Festival of Algiers in 1969, Alboury is not the small barbaric king that colonial history made of him, but a dignified prince who refuses to be suppressed. The play is about the honour of the past. The heroes rise above the historic reality and become glorified, sometimes even deified, giving them an almost mythological status. Such plays, of which most were written in French West Africa, caused a reaction against the William Ponty school of thought. The past had to be honoured again, because

> . . . the African does not come from a historical vacuum. By the reconstruction of his own history faith in the future must be restored.[36]

Chaka is a well-known heroic South African figure, who lived at the start of the nineteenth century. His ambition and military talent made the Zulu people great, but he declined because of egoism, vanity, suspicion and cruelty, and was killed by his own people. The South African, Thomas Mofolo, recorded

a history of Chaka in Sotho which was later translated into English, German and French.

Mofolo's epic in his own language is fascinating,
although it is obvious from many passages that he was
both a Christian and westernised in his thinking. He
succeeded in conveying the many apparent
psychological contradictions in Chaka's character.
Many modern writers were inspired by the story of
the Zulu hero to write free adaptations for the
theatre. Writers like Senghor,[37] Seydou Badian,[38]
Djibril Tamsir Niane,[39] who also translated the
Soundjata epic, and various others have given their
own interpretations to the Chaka legend.

Senghor emphasised the passion and the spirit of
sacrifice of the hero, while Seydou Badian of Mali
chose the theme of his death and draws him as a
black militant fighter. After them Abdou Anta Kâ
wrote his version, called *Les Amazoulous,*[40] in which
Chaka is a visionary who foresees the coming of the
Boers to his land. The Guinean Condetto Nénékhaly-
Camara saw in Chaka the man who moulded a people
into a nation. It needs to be mentioned that his play
Amazoulou,[41] which has an introduction by the
Angolan Mario de Andrade, is dedicated to the
Guinean head of state, Ahmed Sékou Touré, 'revolutionary and friend'. This is perhaps the reason for
the idealisation of the Chaka figure, and the
concealing of his mistakes and paranoia, which are
even transformed where possible to noble heroism.

In the beginning of *Amazoulou* Chaka is called by
the messenger of the gods, the magician Issanoussi. In
the last tableau they meet each other again. At that
stage Chaka is depressed and seems to have lost his
courage to live, but the final dialogue is optimistic
compared to the end of Mofolo's *Chaka.*

Issanoussi: You have great cares. But you still have the power in you to again unite the Zulu people, to be able to face the enormous dangers that the coming of the new conquerors will bring, people with pale skins and cold eyes . . . Do not be disheartened, Chaka. Today we expect in our village the envoys of Moshesh, the prince of the Matabeles. After you he is the mightiest. His support for the Zulu nation will consecrate the grandeur of your work.

Chaka: To tell you the truth, I am tired, dead tired, Issanoussi. And a tired man has to step back . . . What would I have given, Issanoussi, if I could start again in the world of my own dreams!

Issanoussi: You only have to become again the untameable king and fighter. Great deeds await you, compared to which your boldest feats of the past will look small, like the flashing past of fireflies in the night. Think of your name, Chaka, and of the name of your people, Amazoulou, the fire from heaven! That fire scorches the world, from East to West.

Chaka: The thought is too bitter . . .

Messenger: Bayete, o Zulu, Bayete, O king! Bayete, Chaka! I announce the arrival within our walls of the envoys of Moshesh, prince of the Matabeles and the Suthu.

Chaka: Give the order to prepare the festivities . . . We shall celebrate today a rich union. The coming of Moshesh coincides with the beginning of a new era in which the Zulus will protect their blood and their heritage. Have

great fires lit around the village. We are
sealing the new alliance of all Zulus with
their fatherland . . . Do you see Issanoussi, if
Chaka has been great, his people are greater.
We have to warn the people against the
enormous danger that is threatening to en-
gulf them . . . The new battle does not only
concern the people of this land, but all our
people together. And in the last confront-
ation my part will not be small . . .

Issanoussi: The elders know the proverb: 'Stormy today, tomorrow mud and afterwards dried
up, so it is with the deepest water.' No, it is
not so. Living water hollows out the river-
bed. It stretches out and pours itself out to
embrace the land and the mountains and to
weave a protective band that clasps the
universe.[42]

The rejection of the traditional proverb signals the
transformation that will take place in the old society,
a transformation that will be desirable if the people
guard their unity. About Chaka much has been
written and not only for the theatre.[43] In *The
African Image* the South African Ezekiel Mphahlele[44] says,

The Tshaka-figure has always elicited the most heroic
instincts in the African; this in spite of the array of
white historians who have always represented Tshaka,
the Zulu king, as nothing more than a barbarian, a
sadistic savage without a drop of mercy.

In the different Chaka dramas that have been derived
from the original epic the main concern is to use a

historic hero for the restoration of a glorious past and for the termination of colonial rule. Each playwright approaches the hero (others as well as Chaka) in a manner that suits his intentions best. The original hero remains, in the words of Ogunbesan, 'a king for all Seasons.'[45]

STORIES AND FABLES

Playwrights have also used humbler stories and fables from the past. Ama Ata Aidoo of Ghana based *Anowa*[46] on the well-known story of the wilful, pretty girl who refuses all suitors that her parents suggest. She wants to make her own decision and eventually gets married to the devil. The moral of the story is that everyone has to conform to the existing order.

In *Anowa* the authoress has placed an ancient story in the nineteenth century. Kofi, the husband of Anowa, is a trader in hides. By exploiting his slaves he becomes very rich. The wealth, however, makes Anowa unhappy. Her status prevents her from working, because all work is done by slaves. The play ends with Anowa drowning herself and Kofi shooting himself. Their bodies are brought back to Yebi, the town where Anowa was born and to which, after her departure with Kofi, she never wanted to return.

The mother of Anowa represents conventional behaviour which contrasts with the ideas of her obstinate daughter.

> I want my child
> To be a human woman

Marry a man
Tend a farm
And be happy to see her
Peppers and onions grow.
A woman like her
Should bear children
Many children,
So she can afford to have
One or two die.
Should she not take
Her place at meetings
Among the men and women of the clan?
And sit on my chair when
I am gone?[47]

Just as before in the home of her parents, Anowa has her own ideas of marriage. She is against the principle of slave labour through which her husband became rich. There can be no blessing on exploitation. The Old Man, the narrator, says that it is against the 'natural state' of man to make slaves of others and against the will of the gods. Infertility is the result and there will not be anyone to inherit wealth that has been acquired in that way.[48]

Anowa and Kofi Ako are childless. They argue constantly because Anowa refuses to accept her status. During the whole play she wears the same cloth to the annoyance of her husband who behaves like a prince.

Kofi Ako: *(Very angry)* And I do not think there is a
           single woman in the land who speaks to her
           husband the way you do to me. *(Sighs and
           relaxes)* Why are you like this, Anowa?
           Why? *(Anowa laughs)* Can't you be like

other normal women? Other normal people?
(Anowa continues laughing, then stops abruptly)

Anowa: I still do not know what you mean by normal. Is it abnormal to want to continue working?

Kofi Ako: Yes, if there is no need to.

Anowa: But my husband, is there a time when there is no need for a human being to work? After all, our elders said that one never stops wearing hats on a head which still stands on its shoulders.

Kofi Ako: I do not see a reason for me to go walking through forests, climbing mountains and crossing rivers to buy skins when I have bought slaves to do just that for me.

Anowa: And so we come back to where we have been for a long time now. My husband, we did not have to put the strength of our bodies into others. We should not have bought the slaves . . .

Kofi Ako: But we needed them to do the work for us.

Anowa: As though other people are horses! And now look at us. We do nothing from the crowing of the cock to the setting of the sun. I wander around like a ghost and you sit, washed and oiled like a . . . bride on show or a god being celebrated. Is this what we left Yebi for? Ah, my husband, where did our young lives go?[47]

In *Anowa* Ama Ata Aidoo asks questions about poverty, wealth and exploitation which are still relevant in every society today. She does it without the undue emphasis one often finds in literature

which deals with social issues. *Anowa* is beautifully
written and has great dramatic force.

In West Africa, perhaps more than in Eastern,
Central and Southern Africa, there is a whole
tradition of modern dramatisations of old narratives.
This especially applies to Ghana and Nigeria. We have
already referred to the folk opera and the theatre of
people like Ijimere and Ladipo. Soyinka could also be
mentioned here, even though his work shows signs of
many other influences which are discussed in chapter
VII. In Ghana much of modern theatre is based on
the *Anansesem,* the art of narrative as it exists among
the Akan-speaking people. *Anansesem* means 'Ananse
stories', the term indicating both text and performance.

Efua Sutherland of Ghana has developed traditional theatre further in the drama studio at Accra, a
lively centre of theatrical activity.[50] The spider
Ananse is in actual fact a kind of *Everyman*, who
makes people see what they are and what effect
characteristics like avarice, ambition, stupidity or
cleverness can have in a community. The stories are
humorous, but the lessons escape no one. There is a
saying: 'If Ananse is destroyed, the community is
lost'.

The Ananse stories are an instrument for
community criticism in the Akan society. Other
animal stories perform the same function in other
places.

The stories of Ananse's wealth, which he never
acquires honestly and the audience knows he will
never keep for long, are very successful. The narrator
sets the ancient stories in modern context. Many of
the stories from the oral tradition now refer to
money, guns, books, flat-buildings, radios, tele-

vision, trucks and even horse-races or the football
pools.[51] In Efua Sutherland's *The Marriage of
Anansewa*,[52] Ananse's daughter possesses a type-
writer and telegrams are delivered by the postal
services.

The writer leaves the narrator in his omniscient
role. As in ancient times he knows what will happen,
and he intrudes on the action and comments on it. He
also tries to involve the public in the events, mixing
with the audience to elicit their reactions to some
scenes.

In the *Anansesem* there are musical intermezzos,
called *Mboguos.* The narrator can introduce them but
they may also be provided by the voluntary im-
provisation of a member of the audience. The
audience sometimes dances while the music plays.
One of the players may perform a comic solo with
dancing and mime. The *Anansesem* is always introduced by a series of Mboguos, before the narrator can
perform.[53] The singing of the Mboguo is accompanied
by a clapping of hands and a drum rhythm. Such
musical intermezzos have an important position in
The Marriage of Anansewa. Players, musicians,
dancers and singers work together in the place of a
participating audience. The public is no longer willing
to take part. This is a problem which would never
have occurred in the old society.[54]

In the play Ananse tries to marry off his daughter so
that he can profit by it. The girl has to type pretty
letters, dictated to her by her father in flowery
language, but only afterwards does she realise to her
amazement what it is all about. Ananse promises that
he will arrange everything to her satisfaction. Three
of four chiefs to whom Ananse has promised her
hand, and from whom Ananse has already received an

'advance', threaten to come and arrange the marriage. Ananse is in trouble, but at the last moment he finds a clever solution. Anansewa must act as if she is dead when the envoys of the different chiefs come, while Ananse will mourn sadly the sudden death of his only daughter. The only problem is how to get her alive again. Ananse performs a ritual with sacrifices in which the forefathers are invoked. He sings and dances as if he is in a trance. Eventually he succeeds in reviving her, showing how strong was the love between father and daughter. After that Ananse feels justified in giving Anansewa to the fourth chief, the 'Chief-of-Chiefs'. This candidate, who has offered the most, had sent his envoys a bit later then the others, who had already left. Everything is then arranged and the feast can begin. Mboguos form part of various scenes. When the letters are to be sent to the four chiefs (a scene performed with stylised gestures and movements) Anansewa closes the letters. Ananse delivers them at the post office, while he sings, the other players joining in.

Please hurry
For time is nobody's friend.
Hurry,
For time will not wait for you.
Hurry, hurry
Hurry down there.
Hurry, hurry,
Hurry down there.

Time is nobody's friend,
Time is nobody's friend,
Time is nobody's friend.

So hurry, hurry.[55]

An Mboguo is also sung when Ananse does not know what to do. He has hidden himself behind an enormous web in order to think. The narrator and the other players disturb him, and, alternating, they sing,

> Who is knocking?
> Who is knocking?
>
> It is me.
> It is me.[56]

The texts of the songs can easily be learnt by the audience. Besides Efua Sutherland other writers like Martin Owusu have also used Ananse stories for theatrical productions.[57]

Farces are not easily distinguished from the Ananse genre, although the form is different. The farce relies on a rapid sequence of swift actions, without there being opportunity for much singing and dancing. The main concern of the plot is one of pursuit. Someone has to be trapped and thrashed at the end. *The Mirror*[58] by Mukasa-Balikuddembe, who heard the story told in Runyoro/ Rutoro, is an example of this. Similar stories about suspected infidelity have been used as plots for European mediaeval buffooneries and farces. In *The Mirror* we see Bamuroga, his wife Kabuleeta, and a neighbour who intervenes at just the right time in the conjugal dispute. Bamuroga has bought his wife, who has been away to visit her parents, a large mirror as a surprise, the first in the whole village. But when Kabuleeta comes home and looks into the mirror she comes to the wrong conclusion.

Kabuleeta: So, there is another woman in the house. My husband has found someone to replace me in my absence, has he? I'll soon tell her what I think of her. (*She addresses her own reflection*) I can see that you have assumed complete authority in this house. Let me warn you beforehand that I shall not cook under the same roof as a sneaking harlot. You see these cups, these plates, these pots? Well, I bought them with my own money from my mother, and I shall take them back with me. You will have to buy your own.

When an unsuspecting Bamuroga enters, a fight begins, until the misunderstanding is resolved by the neighbour.

It is clear to what extent tradition influenced modern African theatre. An important difference is that now there are more plays written and published in western languages. The western influence has also had the result that the presentations have become more concentrated. In the villages a performance will often last the whole night. City people are no longer accustomed to such leisurely ways. They have found another rhythm of life. In an introduction to a special edition of the magazine *African Literature Today*[59] Eldred Jones says that popular plays are almost never published and that published plays are not always popular with the African public. This statement is especially valid regarding comic one act plays like *The Mirror*, where more depends on the improvising talent of the players than on the written texts.[60] According to Jones the African writer of plays, like other writers, has to contend with a large variety of language and languages from which he has to choose. The 'language of the ear' will have priority with the playwright, who ought to view the publication of his piece as of secondary importance.[61] In practice it is often the other way round. The difference between popular theatre and literary theatre is becoming more and more evident.

FOOTNOTES:

1. Cornevin, 1970.
2. 1966.
3. 1968.
4. 1962.
5. Traore 1967, p 8.
6. Traore 1958 and 1971, Mouralis1971.
7. 1971, p 36.
8. cf Adedeji 1967 and 1971.
9. 1952.
10. 1969, p 188.
11. Hodgkin 1965, pp 29 — 47, Schipper-de Leeuw 1975.
12. 1971, p 45.
13. Ladipo 1964.
14. 1966 and 1969, cf Beier 1973.
15. 1972.
16. 1972.
17. Omara 1972, p 49.
18. 1964.
19. 1966.
20. Laurence 1969, pp 79, 80.

21. Clark 1966, pp 3, 4.
22. Clark 1966, p 121.
23. cf Obiechina 1975, pp 155 ff.
24. Clark 1966, pp 65, 66.
25. Finnegan 1970, pp 111, 112.
26. 1970.
27. Cornevin 1960, p 444.
28. 1968, p 9.
29. cf Nokan 1962 and 1972.
30. 1969 Mushiete and Mikanza 1969: 53.
31. 1973.
32. Salifou 1973, p 13.
33. 1968.
34. 1967.
35. Ndao 1967, p 8.
36. Dailly 1971, p 91.
37. 1964. 38. 1962. 39. 1971. 40. 1972. 41. 1970.
42. Nénékhaly-Camara 1970, pp 92 − 98.
43. E.g. in 1979 Mazisi Kunene published his Zulu epic, *Emperor Shaka the Great*.
44. 1962. 45. 1973. 46. 1973.
47. Aidoo 1973, p 12.
48. Idem, pp 39 − 40.
49. Idem, pp 53 − 54.
50. Sutherland 1972.
51. cf Finnegan 1970, p 387. 52. 1975.
53. cf Clark's Ozidi.
54. Sutherland 1975, pp v − vii.
55. Sutherland 1975, p 9.
56. Idem, p 33.
57. 1973.
58. 1972.
59. 1976.
60. cf Salifou 1973, pp 9, 10.
61. Jones 1976, p 8.

IV. Confrontation
with Colonialism

Strange dawn! The western morning
in black Africa glows with a
smile, the thunder of cannons
and glistening beads . . . It
was a morning of travail[1]

Europe determined the borders of present-day Africa. The division of the continent took place during the Conference of Berlin, from November 1884 to February 1885. There the fourteen interested European countries determined the diplomatic rules for a western monopoly game. Africa was considered to be a continent without leaders.

In African literature one can read about the people's reaction to the coming of the white colonizers, why they opposed or accepted it and what the consequences of colonial domination were for African communities. While reading one realizes that western influence had an enormous impact on African culture. The people's reaction became stronger

as this cultural imperialism grew. More has been
written about this in French than in the English
literature of independent Africa.

In South Africa the colonial situation persists. The
work of banned or imprisoned writers inspired by
events in that country is a repetition of history. The
theme of white domination is almost exhausted in
independent Africa, but in South Africa it is today
more topical than ever.

Colonialism is severely condemned as being in-
human, but in the theatre, just as in the novel, there
are varying views of colonial times: there were good
and bad Europeans, as there were good and bad
Africans, including those who exploited the colonial
situation to better their own positions.

FIRST ACQUAINTANCE

In *The Lands of Kazembe*[2] Masiye of Zambia writes
about the first Portuguese expedition attempting to
find a way from Beira overland to Angola through the
territory of Mwaata Kazembe, the king of the mighty
Luanda empire. The Portuguese leader, Lacerda, dies
in the palace of Kazembe and Angola is never reached.
Masiye remains close to his historic sources, particularly to Lacerda's diary. He illustrates the many
tensions and conflicts such a journey can cause,
not only between Portuguese and Africans, but also
among the Portuguese themselves. The description of
Lacerda is sympathetic. The chief of the Tumbuka
says to him, 'You are a good bwana. Not like bwana
Dombodombo. He talks like a gun.' Dombodombo
means 'terror', the African name for Pereira who took
pride in terrorising Africans with his whip. A note-

worthy fact is that in parts of the play Lacerda is the narrator. The Portuguese expedition is not in Kazembe's interest because he already has his own route to the coast which he does not want taken over by the whites. He uses the death of Lacerda as a pretext to refuse continuation of the voyage. It is 'to their advantage' that they are sent back to Mozambique, otherwise they may all perish.

In his stage directions Masiye says that ideally the play should be performed in a circle, with the audience sitting in the centre. 'In this way the director can show the opposing forces of colonial Beira and Kazembe's autonomous African empire. On the one side of the theatre the Governor General's court is in session, and on the other side Kazembe's, while around the public savannah and bush, through which the expedition is trekking, must be visible'. Communication with the audience must be direct . . .'not only by means of the word, but also by the atmosphere, the terror of the bush and the fear that rules over the Portuguese as well as the African slaves.' In Lusaka the play was performed with success, making use of Zambian dances, music and wherever possible, Nyanja, the local language. This language was used in the dialogues. It is rare that the majority that cannot understand English is considered in this way.[3]

In many cases contact between the colonizers and the local people meant combat. This was the case in battles with the Germans in Cameroon[4] and Tanzania,[5] the Portuguese in Guinea-Bissau,[6] the French in the former French Sudan,[7] the English in Kenya[8] and the white settlers in South Africa,[9] among others. Some heroes of the resistance are Ba Bemba, the king of Sikasso,[10] Lat Dior,[11] Kinjeketile,[12] Samori and his son Karamoko.[13]

This type of theatre is in most cases nothing more than a piece of adapted history, in which most of the people are shallow and schematic. The most interesting are the heroes themselves, the kings, who are reminiscent of their predecessors from the old epics, and the court poets, historians or elders, who are often portrayed on stage. The language is solemn and rich with images. The words of the king are wise and his attitude dignified. Sultan Njoya Moluh in *Les Dieux trancheront*[14] encourages his people before they set out against the white invaders.

The Sultan: Where are the invincible cavaliers, who wage war like a game, a game for men? Where are the men who I have imagined today, dragging along the Bamileke chiefs and their following, capturing and setting up in a row the heads of the Germans?

Everyone: Here we are. Here. We shall overcome.

The Sultan: Last night I consulted the skull of Sultan Moluh. The reply was satisfactory. These were the details: many enemies will be carried away in their flight by the river Lu. I consulted the skull of Mbuembwe, whose garment I wear today. He gnashed his teeth and expressed his regret that he is not alive to share with us this victory, which will be the most important and the quickest in our history *(murmurs of satisfaction)*. The tortoise has been consulted. Many will die, but none or few on our side. The spider moved himself rapidly to my right before I formulated my question.

Everyone: Favourable.
The Sultan: And now, go! And bring back the heads.
                Remember, we are defending our lives, our
                wives, our children, our fatherland and our
                gods. Bring along a calabash with water
                . . . Who can gather streaming water to-
                gether?
Everyone: No one! no one!
The Sultan: No one can collect it. Come closer, grand
                dignitories and princes. *(Each stretches out
                the right hand and the Sultan pours water
                over it.)* Only the dead can break the pact
                instituted by our ancestors . . . Before
                this ground has dried up you will have
                returned victorious.

In *Les Sofas*[15] Bernard Zadi of the Ivory Coast deals
with the problem of the dramatic choice between
fighting to the last man or seeking a compromise with
the stronger whites, thereby saving the people. His
two protagonists defend their own points of view.
Both have valid arguments.

The Sofas form the formidable professional army
of Samory Touré, who wants to construct a new and
mighty country on the ruins of the former Manding
empire. Samory was a controversial figure. He was
without doubt an able general, for years succeeding in
resisting the French, at first in open warfare, and later
with guerilla tactics. He was captured in 1898 and
deported. In the eyes of some he is bloodthirsty and
without respect for human lives. Samory's adversary
is his son Karamoko, who has returned from France.
The young prince realizes better than his father what
the strength of the French invaders is. He suggests
that they make peace, but Samory refuses. Samory's

saying, 'If a man refuses, he says NO,' has become legendary. In a conversation between Samory, his son Karamoko and the wise *dyeli*, Mory Fin'Djan, faithful companion of the king ('the ear of Samory and the voice of the people') the difference of opinions can soon be seen.

Mory: We are listening, prince, and may the truth illuminate your words.

Prince: I do not yet know exactly what happened during my long absence. My father has only briefly told me some things . . . France as I have learnt to know it in four years, that France lives only for peace. Of that I am deeply convinced . . . France wants nothing more than conciliation with the Manding princes. She wants her trade to prosper, and it cannot prosper in time of war. That is the whole meaning of the slogan 'Liberty, Equality, Fraternity'. About that I am also deeply convinced.

Samory: Prince Karamoko, I have to admit to you that I am very worried that the red ears by some magic have confiscated your lion heart in exchange for vain enjoyments. May Allah chastise me if I conceal matters from you while talking to you. But it is as if I am hearing the monotonous prayer of a scholar, repeating what his master says without trying to understand. It is clear that you do not understand the problems of the country.

Prince: *(Indignant)* Father, I cannot bear to be insulted and during this interview.

Samory: *(Rising)* What?

Prince:	Forgive me if I interpret an insult wrongly.
Mory:	Do you still remember, Prince, the stormy night just before your departure overseas, all the battles we fought before we could enforce that famous treaty of Kenieba? Speaking about the French, you said then — and these words have remained famous at the court — The whites? Bah! Souls of slaves. No honour and no word of honour. Real kaffirs. They are so shameless that they alternate songs of peace with songs of war. Do you still remember? Prince, how can you for one moment believe that our mortal enemies would do something in good faith?
Prince:	Since then I have understood that there lies a world between the real French and the murderers who come here on the wings of the devil!

Because of his stay in France Karamoko's thinking had become broader than that of his compatriots who had only experienced the French as occupiers. His father reproaches him that he has soiled himself with the white mentality and, accused of treason, the prince is condemned to death.

THE COLONIAL SYSTEM

European governments colonized Africa, justifying themselves with all sorts of rationalizations. Humane or religious considerations, dedication to the civilization which Europe thought it owed to the rest of the world, stability: all were raised in defence of the colonial system. In fact, the real arguments of the occupier were financial or political. All other matters were subservient to these, merely giving the desire to colonize a noble accent. European colonization of Africa had as its main purpose the gaining of wealth and power.

The colonial situation as experienced by Africans is rendered in plays such as _Béatrice du Congo_[16] by Bernard Dadié of the Ivory Coast, _Simon Kimbangu ou le messie noir_[17] by Philippe Elébé of Zaire, _Oba Waja_[18] by Ladipo, _Death of the King's Horseman_[19] by Soyinka or _Kinjeketile_[20] by Tanzania's Hussein. The central characters in all these plays are historical figures. They are confronted with the prospect of domination by strangers and all become victims of this domination.

Béatrice and Simon Kimbangu both had the guidance of a prophetic movement. Such movements were to the people an expression of their dissatisfaction with the colonial situation. They were a 'substitute for revolution and nationalism and held the promise of a better world that was already beginning with healings and miracles.'[21]

In 1702, in the kingdom of the Congo, a girl named Chimpa Wita was christened by missionaries. After that she was called Béatrice. The girl was serious about her new faith and encouraged her compatriots to live soberly and to renounce their old beliefs. But by her militant interpretation of the Christian message — the Congo was the holy land, Christ was black and a new kingdom was coming in Africa — she damaged the interests of the Portuguese occupier and eventually died on the stake as an 'African Jeanne d'Arc' barely two years after her baptism.[22] Dadié based his _Béatrice du Congo_ on her history. In it he attacked the excesses of the colonial system, telling how the land was stolen and the king led on the leash of the occupier.

Béatrice functions as the conscience of the king. Then he eventually realizes that his coat full of medals and distinctions had been an easy way to bribe him and he offers resistance. He is killed. Christmas is celebrated by a Mass where the whites are carried in sedan chairs by Africans. In the sermon, they are told that they have to be subservient to authority and accept their suffering the way Jesus accepted his . . . ²³ Two centuries later the prophet Simon Kimbangu almost had the same fate. He was a student of the Protestant mission in the Belgian Congo and he opposed certain kinds of dancing and fetishism. He attained great authority by his healing of the sick, and there were rumours that he restored the dead to life. In his play Elébé makes the colonial administration, the Catholic church and Capital responsible for the arrest of Kimbangu, who moved among the people like a black messiah and often repeated exactly the words and deeds of Jesus. The Protestant missionary Jennings (obviously not a Belgian) is sympathetic towards Kimbangu and is himself looked upon with suspicion by the representatives of the church, the king and the colony. The Catholic church starts to lose members and people leave their work to follow Kimbangu en masse. The authorities look for Kimbangu in his town, Nkambe, where chief Mbemba is called up to answer to Morel, the administrator. Morel tries in vain to get the African on his side.

Morel: Kimbangu is working against the Mbula-
           Matari. He is preventing others from going

	to work. He acts as if he were sent by God, but he wants to take your place.
Mbemba:	Kimbangu is solely occupied with his teaching. He has also healed many sick people.
Morel:	*(Furious)* Do you believe in Kimbangu?
Mbemba:	The whole village is in favour of Kimbangu. I cannot do anything about it.
Morel:	Just tell me where he hides. Nothing will happen to him.
Mbemba:	I am not able to tell you where Kimbangu is hiding.
Morel:	Then you are against the Mbula-Matari. Do you know what that means?
Mbemba:	The pastor and the priest talk about God, and that Kimbangu also does. He teaches us what he has learnt from the Protestants. Kimbangu has taught us that we blacks and the whites are brothers, because we have the same father.

(Morel in anger leaves with his soldiers. Mbemba sits on his throne and calls his narrator who plays his instrument at the feet of his chief):

Narrator:	Ee e, e, e, iyaleeh!
	He comes from far,
	the white man
	carrying
	a gun and
	a crucifix . . .
	E, e, e, e, iyaleeh!
	the white man,
	the man with nine evils,
	has made life difficult for us.
	E, e, e, e, iyalee!

> Spirits of the forefathers,
> Punish the white man,
> the man with nine evils.
> Let the lightning strike his house!
> Iyaleeh, o, o, o, . . .[24]

Kimbangu is betrayed by a compatriot and arrested. During the trial the death sentence is passed but this is later commuted to life imprisonment. The main charge against him is that he 'infused the indigenous population with wrong religious ideas by which they were incited against the established order'.[25]

Charged with xenophobia and assailing the public order thousands of Kimbangu's followers are deported. Later, during the fifties, the separatist religious movements lose power with the rising of nationalistic parties.[26]

Religious sects and prophetic movements arise wherever people are suppressed. Such movements are not necessarily Christian-inspired. *Kinjeketile*[27] takes place in Tanzania and tells of a prophet who is possessed by a water spirit, Hongo. To unify the people of different tribes against the common enemy, he uses water as symbol. *Maji* (water in Kiswahili) will make the people strong to destroy the Red Earth (the Germans). They are suffering under a forced labour system, the whip of the cruel white overseer and the compulsory tax being paid to the strangers who have taken their country. Kinjeketile tries in vain to postpone the battle, because *maji*, (unity in this case) is not yet strong enough. Now no one is listening. Trusting that maji will make them immune to the bullets of the enemy they attack the German fort. Many are killed and Kinjeketile is captured. The Germans order him to declare that the story of the water is false, but he refuses. Some day it will become reality. In this play Hussein uses war dances, rites and songs, but also different kinds of language. Kinje-ketile for instance speaks quite differently in normal life than he does when in a trance. His speeches are full of poetic images and, in his vision, gods, man and nature form a unity.

In many countries the colonial authority collaborated with the mission from the mother country. Converted Africans were often accused by relatives of being on the side of the occupier. In the Kenyan, Kenneth Watene's *My Son for My Freedom*[28] a choice has to be made between Christianity and the Mau Mau.

Because the colonizers do not understand the old traditions conflicts regularly arise between the population and authority. Becoming involved, the whites might aggravate troubled situations. In *Oba waja* ('The king is dead') a story based on a real incident, by Duro Lapido,[29] two people are killed when the district commandant tries to save one life. The people of Oyo lament:

White man, bringer of new laws,
White man, bringer of new times,
Your work was confounded by Eshu, confuser of men.
Nobody can succeed against the will of Eshu,
The god of fate.
Having thrown a stone today, he kills a bird yesterday
Lying down, his head hits the roof.
Standing up, he cannot look into the cooking-pot.
With Eshu
Wisdom counts for more than good intentions
And understanding is greater than justice.[30]

The same theme was used by Soyinka in *Death and the King's Horseman.*[31]

ASSIMILATION

In his *Portrait du colonisé*[32] Memmi describes two possible answers of the colonised to his situation: assimilation or protest.

The tendency towards assimilation arises because of the need to break the mental bondage of the colonial situation. The colonizer is imitated as far as possible in his language, his customs and his mentality. The colonized seeks acceptance in the fact that he does everything exactly as the whites do. He wants to become 'as white as possible'. Obama from the Cameroons calls one of his plays *Assimilados.*[33] *The Blinkards* is a comedy by the Ghanaian writer Sekye that satirizes the nouveaux-rich among the Fanti. They have felt it necessary to accept the social and cultural consequences of colonialism. But eventually some sceptical adversaries succeed in removing the 'blinkards' from the eyes of some imitation whites. The moral is clear, and the exaggerated imitation of the whites becomes hilarious. Mrs Brofusem for example wears a pince-nez. She wants her husband to call her 'my little duckling' (she had heard an Englishman calling his wife that) and she wants to kiss him. This gives the servant a fright as he thinks she wants to bite her husband. The men in the play wear tropical helmets, closed shoes and gloves. The return to sandals at the end of the play is a revolutionary act in the minds of the Brofusem couple. Although this play is set in another time the African audience will recognize in it relatives and friends who still believe that overseas products, manners, and attitudes must be better than those of their own country.

Monsieur Thôgô-gnini[34] delves deeper into the consequences of assimilation. The name of the main character means in Malinke 'someone who wants to make a name at any cost'. It takes place during 1840 somewhere on the west coast of Africa. Thôgô-gnini is a liberated slave returning from America to his country where he becomes an intermediary between the white traders and the Africans. He enriches himself while the Africans working under the supervision of whites on the plantations earn practically nothing. Thôgô-gnini rejects his own past and becomes more and more westernized. He admires the whites, their land and everything coming from it. He very much wants a street in France named after him, and he wants a mass for his late father to be read in a church in the land of the whites.

> First white: You want a mass read at our place in memory of your father who died in Africa?
> Thôgô-gnini: Yes, I have to tell you that he died without having the opportunity of becoming white . . .
> First white: Becoming white?
> Thôgô-gnini: Through baptism . . . [35]

Monsieur Thôgô-gnini illustrates the circumstances surrounding the meeting between white and black in Africa. A few privileged Europeans and a handful of assimilated Africans exploit the rest of the population and the characteristic traits of the colonizer are often perpetuated by the 'new elite'.

There is a scene in the play where Thôgô-gnini is

molested by some of his victims. In a scene almost without dialogue they tie him up, paint his face and hands white, redden his lips and hang ornaments round his neck and on his ears. Then they force him to dance and again tie him to his chair. They force him to smell his money before removing trunks of it. Thôgô-gnini remains behind with a board on his stomach on which his captors had written the beginning of a well-known European proverb, EVERY MAN FOR HIMSELF . . . , a proverb that also applies increasingly to Africa, especially to urban Africans. This play has been performed with great success in Africa.

PROTEST

Something of the second answer of the colonized has already been heard in plays such as *Béatrice du Congo*, *Kinjeketile* and *Oba Waja*. Memmi[36] makes it clear that the assimilated, after unsuccessful attempts at acceptance by the ruling group, realize that imitation gains them nothing. The whites will always treat them as second class citizens. Often it is because of this experience that they choose protest as an answer to their position.

The subject of *Aube Africaine* by the Guinean, Keita Fodeba, is the transition from assimilation to an awareness of the worth of his own culture. The Malian, Naaman, is enlisted to serve in the colonial army. He shows the whites how brave Africans can be. He is even decorated by his white superiors. Then he is wounded and becomes a German prisoner.

The sad news lies on the village with its whole weight.

All through the night war drums are heard, while the
assembly of Notables, in traditional dress, decides that
Naaman will have to dance the *Douga*, the holy dance of
the *Vulture*, the dance of the Manding princes of which
each step is a stage in the History of Mali.[37]

No one is allowed to do this dance without having
performed a deed of heroism and importance to the
community. Only later on does Naaman become
aware of the contradictory nature of his actions. He
will never be liberated by fighting on the side of the
colonial army. On the way back from the front the
Africans come into conflict with the white military
authorities. Naaman is shot and buried in the town of
Thiaroye in Senegal.

CORA MUSIC

. . . the dawn had come . . . the dawn of African freedom.
The first rays of sunlight hardly touch the surface of the
sea, giving to the white waves of foam a golden glow.
The palms bend in the soft morning breeze, saddened by
this early battle, their stems facing the ocean. Noisy
flocks of crows come screeching about the tragic events
that have coloured red the dawn of Thiaroye . . . And in
the red-glowing blue, just above the body of Naaman, a
large vulture hovers in the sky. It seems as if it is saying
to him, Naaman, you have not danced the holy dance
with my name. In liberating the African Fatherland
others will dance the *Douga*.[38]

African Dawn — more of a musical narration than a
western style play — has been cited as an example of
good *littérature engagée,* among others by Frantz
Fanon in *Les damnés de la terre.*[39] The colonized

were used as soldiers to fight in both wars for the liberation of their European overlords, and because of this they were often indoctrinated to such an extent that they could be used against the country's liberation movements. In our time this is happening in Namibia and South Africa. It is apparent from the history of that country that a colonial situation exists in South Africa.

Here too the colonized try to be assimilated or else they protest. From within that colonial situation the oppressed in South Africa write and perform — perform more than write, because what is not written on paper is less easy to censure. *Revolution* by Leshoai[40] and *The Rhythm of Violence* by Lewis Nkosi[41] are plays of this kind.

Leshoai situates his play in a white church in Bloemfontein. Sebetsa comes into the church with an elderly white priest. In his hand he has a pail of water, a mop, a brush and a piece of green soap. It is the day before Christmas and the church needs to be cleaned. When the African is on his knees with his pail an angry white policeman comes into the church, thinking that the black man is praying. After a long stream of abuse to which Sebetsa reacts humbly with 'ja baas' and 'dankie baas' the policeman realizes that the African is only scrubbing the floor. He leaves and Sebetsa on his knees thanks God. The priest comes back, and in his turn he reproaches Sebetsa because he is praying.

Priest: What are you praying for when you should be scrubbing this floor? You people are lazy and can never be trusted for a few minutes.

Sebetsa: *(Peeved)* I was thanking God for having

	saved my life.
Priest:	What do you mean?
Sebetsa:	I mean saving my life from a bloody Boer policeman brother of yours who wanted to kill me!
Priest:	*(Screaming)* Boy, do not use dirty language in this church. And why did he want to kill you?
Sebetsa:	*(Screaming)* Don't scream at me in church! He wanted to kill me when he walked in here, he thought I was praying.
Priest:	*(Screaming)* Shut your mouth! Who are you not to be screamed at in church? If you were not praying what were you doing?
Sebetsa:	*(Advancing angrily)* Just scrubbing this bloody floor to make it clean for white knees.
Priest:	The devil strike you dead for your insolence.[42]

Then the tension becomes too great for Sebetsa, he forgets his subservient position and starts throwing hymn books at the priest. He hits him with a mass bell, shouting 'blood, war, revolution', until the white man lies dead on the floor.[43]

The desire for social change, but in a more organised form, also rules the younger ones in Nkosi's *The Rhythm of Violence.* Here a racially mixed group at the start of the sixties plants a bomb in the Johannesburg city hall. Despite some melodrama because of too much emphasis on interracial relations, the events in this play clearly cast a light on a new phase in protest in South Africa.[44]

FOOTNOTES:

1. Kane, 1961, p 65.
2. 1973.
3. Masiye 1973, p vii.
4. Kayor 1971.
5. Hussein 1970.
6. Alkaly 1972.
7. Niane 1971.
8. Watene 1973.
9. Leshoai 1972.
10. Niane 1971.
11. Dia 1965.
12. Hussein 1970.
13. Ndao 1973, Zadi 1975.
14. Kayor 1971, pp 72, 73.
15. 1975.
16. 1970.
17. 1972.
18. 1967.
19. 1975.
20. 1970.
21. Schipper 1970, p 31.
22. Balandier 1965, 261 ff, Kaké 1969.
23. Dadié 1970, 119 ff.
24. Elébé 1972, pp 49, 50.
25. Ibid, p 163.
26. Schipper 1970, p 31.
27. Hussein 1970.
28. 1973.
29. Lapido 1967.
30. Ibid, p 166.
31. 1975 cf Chapter vii in this book.
32. 1966.
33. 1972.

34. Dadié 1970.
35. Ibid, pp 65, 66.
36. 1966.
37. Fodeba 1965, p 77.
38. Fodeba 1965, p 77.
39. 1961.
40. 1972.
41. 1964.
42. Leshoai 1973, pp 38, 39.
43. Ibid, p 41.
44. Apronti 1976.

V. Tradition and Change

Every society, even the most traditional, continually undergoes a process of change. Many playwrights are interested in the contrast between the traditional and the modern in terms of the generation conflict where young and old confront each other.

The writer attributes certain convictions to his characters. Where he takes sides it is normally on the side of the younger generation.[1] He wants to demonstrate to his audience that the young are not necessarily wrong because they are young. Often, on the other hand, he will revive ancient values that ought not to be lost. Here also it is evident that the playwright, like the traditional narrator, tries to persuade the public that he is right. Generally the clarity of his message leaves nothing to be desired. He chooses to support or oppose the norms that govern society, whether they are existing taboos, traditional circumcision, tribalism, marriage and dowry, or emancipation.

BREAKING THE TABOO

In *La Marmite de Koka-Mbala*[2] the Congolese Guy
Menga shows young people breaking down a
dangerous taboo in a closed traditional community
where there is no western influence. In the kingdom
of Koka-Mbala certain laws have become merciless
instruments of power, by which the elders rigorously
controlled the morals of the young, while among
themselves they applied these laws more flexibly.

During the reign of king Bitsamou the situation
reaches a climax when Bobolo, the first councillor of
the king and also witchdoctor and fetish priest,
instals a 'cooking pot of spirits' to keep people in his
power. In this pot, according to him, there are the
spirits of the ancestors who see to it that all the laws
of the kingdom are strictly adhered to and applied.
Whenever the council of notables and the king
hesitate to pronounce the death sentence on allegedly
immoral young ones the fetish priest places the pot in
their midst, so that they accept the death sentence
out of fear of the ancestors. Then, one night, the king
has an anxious dream which leads him to reflect on
the course of events. He and Bobola become alienated.
With the aid of his wife, Lemba, king Bitsamou
prevents the persecution of Bitala by the fetish priest.
Bitala, a young man, has been caught while secretly
watching a woman bathing. He is exiled, and during
his exile Bitala discovers that laws in other countries
are less severe. Secretly he returns to Koka-Mbala to
prepare an 'action' with other young people. One day
they penetrate into the palace while the king and his
notables are having a meeting. Bitala demands the
retirement of the hesitant notables and the
destruction of the spiritual cooking-pot. An end has

to be made to the suppression of young people.

King: Young man, I admire your temerity and your brave spirit. But do not forget that this pot is holy and cannot just be broken as if it were an ordinary piece of kitchen ware.

Bitala: Do not be naive, your Majesty. This pot has nothing sacred about it. It is only an instrument of mystification, invented by a person with boundless ambition, to make fools of people. As long as the pot is present while you are deliberating neither you nor your councillors will be able to speak or act freely, because your conscience is bound to it. Your Majesty, for the last time, give the order that the pot is to be broken.

(Silence. All eyes are riveted on the pot. The king hesitates)

Bobolo: Well then, gentlemen. Do what you like. Break the pot, if you are convinced that there is nothing in it. Why are you waiting? . . . Ah . . . Ah . . . Ah . . . No one says anything? No one has the courage. The fear of death nails you to the floor even now, Sire. Sacred pot, no one doubts your power. Let me take you back to your temple.

(He advances on the pot)

King: Guards, arrest this man. And to prove that the king is not afraid, neither of the power of the pot, nor of death, I order you, Bitala, to break this pot.[3]

In this play it is not the concern of the younger generation to usurp parental authority. The Kikongo proverb quoted by Bitala says, 'It does not matter how big they are, the ears never protrude above the head.' Only an excess of authority leads to protest. In *The Cooking-pot of Koka-Mbala* the audience feels the terror created by the medicine man, Bobolo, but at the same time its members are dissociated from it. The fetish priest is an incarnation of authoritarian power-lust which is rejected in this traditional community.

Almost the same pattern is followed by the Nigerian, Henshaw, in *This Is Our Chance*.[4] Here a community that is burdened by antiquated traditions is described. The community wants to adopt some western values, but for the chief — Damba — the entire tradition is sacred. Those who wish to change any part of the social structure are seen as sacrilegious. During the course of the play Damba begins to realize that his view of tradition is not completely correct.[5]

In *The Married Bachelor*[6] the theme is the opposing opnions of the father and Denis, his son. The difference has resulted from the son's education. Denis teaches African culture at the university of Nairobi. Although he tells his students how bad it is that the sacred African culture is being contaminated by foreign elements, his personal life is not in agreement with what he teaches. His son, Yohana, is being educated by his grandparents in a village because Denis is a widower. When the young one has to be circumcised the grandfather wants it done in the traditional manner while Denis prefers to take his son to hospital.

Agala: He is mad. To a hospital indeed. Whose grand-

son will he take to a hospital? . . . I will teach
him to respect me. I will make him learn that
I am the lord of this house. Yohana will be
circumcised here and nowhere else. He will be
circumcised by that same knife that worked
on his ancestors. His warm blood must trickle
into the soil that now covers the skeletons of
his dead forefathers. I will not have this
blood swept away from the floors of a hospital. If I fail in this, I raise my fingers to the
skies, I am not Makonde's son.[7]

When Denis comes to discuss the affair he eventually
yields to the wish of his father, but he refuses,
because of his work in the city, to come to the village
fourteen days after the circumcision to wash his son.
According to tradition this has to be done by the
father. Denis breaks the rule and Yohana dies shortly
after the circumcision. Agala goes to the city to
tell his son that a curse rests on him. He is guilty of
his son's death.

Denis's attitude is not consistent. In the city he
argues with his westernized students for the preserv-
ation of African culture, more a fashionable view-
point than a conviction. In his attitude towards the
people in town he does not maintain his western or
his African views. Against his will he allows the
circumcision to take place, but does not adhere to
the prescriptions.

AMBIVALENT BEHAVIOUR

There is something ambiguous in an attitude that at
one moment renounces tradition and at the moment

of need returns to it. At school and at university students have often sought magical aids when the risk of failing their examinations becomes a reality. Businessmen and ministers sometimes try to improve their positions by consulting a traditional doctor. To increase material prosperity or to prolong life, urbanised people will sometimes seek the help of traditional methods. In a piece by Efua Sutherland, *Edufa* has to sacrifice the life of his wife in order to live longer. Through his uncertainty Edufa seeks an impossible compromise and he brings evil to his own house.

In *The Sudden Return* by the Ghanaian, Martin Owusu Kojo, Tabi sells the lives of his wife and children to a *Mallam*, a witch-doctor, in exchange for personal riches. This story-line refers to the common belief in the power of spirits who can be bribed by human sacrifice. Tabi is prepared to sacrifice his wife and two children.

Mallam: Ah? All? You want a lot of money, ah?

Tabi: I mean, I don't want the children to be motherless and my wife will be unhappy all her life without the children.

Mallam: I understand. Give me their names. Wife first and then the children . . . Wait! Whisper into my ears. Aha-aha-tau! Kneel here. Hold this knife and then bring it down. You pierce the white cloth with the knife . . . into the bowl . . . three times. The first for your wife, the second for your elder daughter, the third for the last born.

Tabi: I understand . . .

Mallam: Here we go . . . *(He closes his eyes and whispers incantations over the bowl. He raises his*

> *hands slowly, getting more involved in his concentration. He lowers his hands sharply. This is done three times, each time piercing the cloth. After each stab there is an awful scream of pain.)* Did you hear the scream?

Tabi: What scream?

Mallam: You did not hear three screams?

Tabi: No.

Mallam: You are not only blind, you are deaf as well. The work is done. I saw your three victims come into the bowl, innocent and helpless. Each time you pierced the heart and the scream followed. But you have no eyes.

Tabi: Well?

Mallam: It is done. Every year for three years one of your victims will die. The deaths will seem very ordinary, nothing mysterious. Each additional death will add a fortune to your wealth. That will also come to you naturally.[9]

The story of Tabi, who leaves his town for fifteen years and returns full of remorse, to find a desolate situation there, has a sound dramatic structure. Traditional elements such as songs, proverbs and rituals are integrated into the form of a modern play.

A too-forced transition from tradition to a westernized existence can lead to serious crises in the lives of younger people, as the Kenyan, Watene, demonstrates in *The Haunting Past.*[10] The problem of the treatment of the spiritually ill in Africa is the theme of *Pinthioum Fann*[11] by the Senegalese, Abdou Anta Kâ, who was treated in a mental hospital in Dakar. The western approach to the African way of thinking often hinders recovery.

TRIBALISM

In 1972 Abdou Anta Kâ's adaptation for the stage of
the novel *Gouverneurs de la roseé* [12] by the Haitian,
Jacques Roumain, appeared. Here the historical
hatred between two clans plays a major role, illustr-
ating how such enmity obstructs the development of
the people.[13]

In modern African society tribalism is often
manifest. Matters as diverse as fights with neighbours
and political decisions, might all have the same root.
Playwrights are bound to give attention to it.

The Kenyan Ngugi wa Thiong'o (James Ngugi)
wrote *The Black Hermit*[14] on the occasion of the
Uhuru celebrations for Ugandan independence in
1962 because the people wanted something different,
a break with the past. Ngugi explains in a preface that
he was at that stage convinced that tribalism was the
major problem of the new East African states:

> I, along with my fellow undergraduates, had much faith
> in the post-colonial governments. We thought they
> genuinely wanted to involve the masses in the work of
> reconstruction. After all, weren't the leaders themselves
> sons and daughters of peasants and workers? All the
> people had to do was to co-operate. All we had to do
> was to expose and root out the cantankerous effects of
> tribalism, racialism and religious factions.[15]

The Black Hermit, a play in three acts, illustrates
something of this belief and also of the impossibility
of turning time back. The younger ones do not want
to be bound to the family. Remi, the central
character, is the first and only one from his town who
has studied at university. The people of his own town

expect him to occupy a leading position.

They regard him as a kind of Moses who is going to free them from misery. But Remi is an irresolute person who hesitates for a long time between the binding tribal laws and an anonymous existence in the city with his white friend, Jane. One of his problems is his aversion towards the obligation to marry the childless widow of his brother. His antipathy towards this obligation is even greater because he once liked this woman, Thonie, but she discarded him for his brother. He now refuses her, and he does it with such cruelty that Thonie has no other way out but to commit suicide. Gradually he realizes that he has isolated himself, like a hermit, from the village community.

Leader: Elders, I know you all want Remi to come back.

Elders: Yes, Remi must come back.

Leader: I am not making a speech. But a word, one word that I must share with you. We elders of Merua love our soil. Because we love that soil, we, years ago, agreed to fight the white man and drive him away from the land. Today the same love of our soil makes us turn to the only educated man in the country. Look at our country since independence. Where is the land? Where is the food? Where are the schools for our children? Who of our tribe is in the government? Who of our flesh and blood can be seen in long cars and houses built of stone? Our tribe waits under a government composed of other tribes. What has Uhuru brought us?[16]

Remi is called back to town, but he brings with him a friend of another tribe and hand in hand they confront the people. Tribalism has to disappear, they say. The National Party will change everything. Some elders leave, hurt or shamed, but most of the people remain, and together they sing the National Anthem before they disperse.

> Remi: And remember what I told you. We must all
>   turn to the soil. We must help ourselves, build
>   more schools, turn our hearts and minds to
>   create a nation, then will tribe and race
>   disappear. And man shall be free . . . [17]

This is one aspect of *The Black Hermit*. It is also about racism, religious oppositions and problems of relationships. Perhaps because of the multiplicity of themes the play is not convincing. The use of language is often bad and the characters are generally not well drawn. Often tribalism is the theme of a play about an inter-tribal love affair that the parents try to prevent, but the lovers struggle to maintain.

MARRIAGE AND DOWRY

In both *Dear Parent and Ogre*[18] and *The New Patriots*[19] by Sarif Easmon of Sierra Leone, tribalism is the cause of troubles between parents, especially fathers and children. In the former, Dauda wants to force his daughter into a marriage, because it will be to his political advantage. The 'Yalie' which his daughter, Siata, has chosen belongs, according to Dauda, to an inferior clan. The father prides himself on his noble tribe and aristocratic origins.

Dauda: *(Suppressing his anger)* You come of a tribe, child, where parents arrange marriages, and the children gratefully go on the honeymoon! Besides, in our family, so long used to rule in the past, the young women have always considered themselves honoured when they were married to strengthen their fathers' kingdoms.

Siata: That's all rubbish . . .

Dauda: My god! Has not democracy turned this Africa upside down? All my ancestors must turn in their graves to hear my own daughter talk to me so.

Siata: If they had any sense, they'd applaud . . . You men have a choice: either you keep us women in harems or send us to the university. If you only wanted a cow, instead of a daughter, to cross with the first bull you thought fit to bring along, then, dear Daddy, you should have kept me away from books. Marry Mahmoud indeed! Hah! What next?[20]

In *The New Patriots* the theme is similar. When minister Byeloh discovers that his daughter has an affair with a creole he is beside himself. 'She has shamed the tribe.'[21]

Easmon as well as De Graft[22] direct themselves to the older generation with a plea in favour of the new ideas of the young. They are both from West Africa, but these problems are found wherever communities are beginning to lose their isolated characters. In Ruanda it is Naigiziki who in *L'optimiste*[23] has the Hutu, Jules, marry the Tutsi girl, Monica. Here the author makes it clear that the youth is right and there will be a happy ending. The young people can no

longer identify themselves with the small world of
the clan. They want a national rather than tribal
perspective. The differences are more complicated
when they concern relationships between people
from different countries or of different races.[24]

The work of the Cameroon writer Guillaume
Oyono-Mbia[25] is critical of tradition, but his fame
rests mainly on his satires and the comic procédés,
such as exaggeration, repetition and contrast, that he
uses. *Trois prétendants . . . un mari*[26] concerns the
African tradition of the dowry, the ancient custom
that the groom gives a present to the family of the
bride. The gift can be anything: cattle, money or
food. Sometimes the suitor of the daughter also has
to work for a while on the land of the prospective
bride's family. The marriage present has for ages been
an important institution in Africa and such traditions
do not suddenly disappear. Modern girls object to the
dowry when they feel they are being traded to the
highest bidder. A girl with schooling is likely to be
married off to an older, richer man who has various
other wives. In the discussion her opinion has little
influence. It is the family that decides.

In his play *Trois prétendants . . . un mari,* Oyono-
Mbia defends the rights of the woman who wants to
marry the man of her choice. This work has been
performed successfully in Africa and Europe. The
action takes place in Mvoutessi, a little village in the
bush. The central character, Juliette, returns home
for the school holidays to hear that her marriage
has been arranged without her having seen her future
husband. A first candidate had offered a hundred
thousand francs, but a second, an important official,
is prepared to double that. When Mbia, the official,
arrives in his large Mercedes the sound of his arrival

causes great excitement in the family. All the men have converged in front of the house of Atangana, the father, to be present when Mbia officially asks for the hand of Juliette. Most of those present make use of the opportunity to tell Mbia what they want, gifts varying from a tergal costume to a transistor radio or an English bicycle. Naturally the high official promises to see to all their needs. The village rejoices while the two hundred thousand francs are being given to Atangana. The agreement is concluded. Mbia will receive Juliette, and she will be his ninth wife, the only educated one. After a long discussion and several bottles of wine the chief of the village addresses the people:

Mbarga: Everyone listen to me! I am the chief! Mbia, the high official you see here, has come from Sangmélima to marry our daughter Juliette. I know that some among us think that there are family connections between him and Juliette, and that marriage is therefore impossible. But what does it matter? Can we refuse a marriage to a high official because of such reasons? Shouldn't we treat important people with consideration?

Everyone: That is true.

Mbarga: Who will receive us every time we go to the city?

Everyone: He will.

Mbarga: Who will give us food and drink, as the whites have it, in the grand restaurants of Sangmélima?

Everyone: He alone.

Mbarga: Who will deliver us from the commissioners and from the police?

Everyone: Yé é é! No one else but he.

Mbarga: Who knows? Is it not so that Mbia will give us authorization for the purchase of arms and medals?

Everyone: He will do it . . . arms . . . medals.

Mbarga: Will Mbia not see to it that we will be able to enter into the administrative offices of Sangmélima, even at the Prefect, without having to wait?

Everyone: Without having to wait?

Mbia: *(Negligently)* Engulu! A bottle of wine for the chief!

Mbarga: Who in this town does not know my great wisdom?

Everyone: Everyone knows it.

Mbarga: How could we refuse a marriage to such a great man? A man of whom the whole of Sangmélima talks, and whom I have so often seen in the company of the minister?

Mbia: *(Flattered)* Engulu! Two bottles for the chief!

Mbarga: Who will soon be mayor?

Mbia: Four bottles!

Mbarga: Parliamentarian?

Mbia: Engulu! Ten bottles!

Mbarga: Minister?

Mbia: Engulu! . . . A case of red wine for the chief.[27]

The scene is in some ways reminiscent of Molière. Juliette is the one person who has not been taken into consideration. Stubbornly she refuses to marry Mbia, and amazes everyone by saying that she is already engaged to a school friend from another district. She does not tell them that she has already brought him to the village to introduce him to her family. She steals the dowries of both candidates, altogether an amount of three hundred thousand francs. In this way the promises to the former suitors are redeemed and she imagines that she will be able to marry her beloved.

The theft is soon discovered and the family is desperate, especially when Mbia threatens them with police action. Desperately Atangana plans to take his daughter to Yaoundé to present her to all the ministers and to give her to anyone who offers the three hundred thousand francs with which to compensate the two suitors. Into this panic Oko, her beloved, arrives, grandly dressed in traditional Bamum costume and accompanied by six musicians playing the *balafong*. This stranger declares himself prepared to marry Juliette and money is no problem to him, but his only condition is that she herself says what she thinks about it.

Mbarga: Must we ask her to say 'yes'? Imagine, perhaps she will say no! Ah. Kouma, can you please explain to the Doctor that women have no say here in Mvoutessi. We have decided to give Juliette to him. What does she have to say about it?[28]

The play ends with a feast where everyone dances, actors as well as audience. Oyono Mbia says he aimed at as much audience participation as possible. The audience must sing and move spontaneously. The fact that he succeeded in getting audience involvement in Europe, and even in England, was especially pleasing to him.

EMANCIPATION

Oyono Mbia justly remarks in the preface to *Trois prétendants* that he does not moralize intentionally. When people are being amused the lesson comes naturally. That is one of the reasons why Mbia has written excellent theatre. Nonetheless Oyono Mbia is considered by the girls in his country as the 'champion of the liberation of the African woman'.[29] Girls see themselves in Juliette, and like the heroine of *Trois prétendants . . . un mari* they reject the submissiveness of the women of earlier generations. For the first time they feel that they have the right to criticize the existing order.

We have already seen how Siata[30] tells her father the truth, and the girl Mahmeh[31] tells her father that he and she are talking to each other from different sides of the century.[32] Denis's friend Mary goes to meetings on the liberation of women[33] and Nokan presents the girl Fatouma and calls her a *jeune fille 'lettrée', très emancipée.*[34] In *Continent-Afrique* the *Récitante* pulls off her veil, and says,

> With this my suffering ends. The pain that I have had to bear all the long ages of suffering and sadness has produced a fruit that has the taste of dawn. I have brought forth a new world.[35]

Most often the African writer shows the conservative authority as opposing women's striving for liberty. The writer's sympathy is almost always with women who are trying to improve their position in society.[36] In practice the attainment of equal rights is difficult. Parental authority is strong and most young men would prefer to retain authority in their homes.

Young men all want to marry virgins and women are expected to be faithful to their husbands. But for themselves the men have quite different norms. This is the experience of Mary who lives with her friend, Denis. When she tells him that she already has a child by someone else he chases her away, even though he has a son. Mary says that she is in the same situation as he is, but Denis does not agree.

Denis: You are a woman. I am a man. You have once been pregnant. I have not. Do you still believe us to be similar?

Mary: But the basic facts are the same.

Denis: Basic facts? What do you know about basic facts? The trouble with women is that you listen to the preaching of some western intellectual, talking about the equality of men and women and you imagine he is right. What you fail to realize is that a woman is danger-ously handicapped. This calls for more restriction of her physical desires. Women must exercise greater control over themselves if they are to retain their dignity in society. Right now yours, if you had any, has vanished into thin air.

Mary: Please, Denis, be kind. You are hurting me. Please.

Denis: I am not hurting you. You hurt yourself the moment you allowed a man to share a blanket with you, give you a child and get away with it.[36]

Women may indeed adopt something of the western woman's drive for liberation, but it is also true that modern African society mirrors that of the west in some respects. The typical western concepts of male and female professions have been adopted by African countries. The first professions for educated women were those of teachers and nurses. In government and commerce women were thought of as suited only to being telephonists, typists or secretaries. The same happened in education. Girls received less training and that which they did receive was more of a domestic than of a technical nature.[37] The fact that most of the plays discussed so far have been written by men is also a reflection of social relationships.

Two East African writers who are consciously working towards social change need to be mentioned.[38] Peninah Muhando of Tanzania writes in Kiswahili, which is spoken in large parts of East and Central Africa, in order to reach a wide audience. Her subject matter is political oppression[39] and the problems of the unmarried pregnant girl in the city.[40]

Rebecca Njau of Kenya, wrote *The Scar*[41] and *In the Round Chain*.[42] Both plays are concerned with justice for oppressed groups.

The theme of *The Scar* is the oppression of the woman in rural Kikuyu society. Mariana, a leading figure in the town, has revolutionary ideas. She tries to liberate the women from senseless practices like the circumcision of girls and from the tribal superstitions that keep them suppressed. The older women distrust her, but Mariana succeeds to a small extent in making girls and young women aware of new possibilities. Eventually she has to leave the town when it becomes known that she was raped at sixteen and has a daughter. Mariana fights for the improvement of women's position in society.

I want them to free themselves from slavery,
I want them to respect their bodies and minds,
I want them to break away the chains
that have so long bound them.[43]

Many more prejudices and obstacles will have to be removed before this wish can be fulfilled.

Sometimes when a community no longer sees them as being of value certain traditional rules become vulnerable to influences for change.[44] In a closed community with little influence from outside social equilibrium is not necessarily disturbed by such changes. The risk is greater when traditions stop being important to a community. This happens in the cities where the whole social structure is crumbling. African cities are a mixture of local and western elements, of screaming advertising and grey misery, modern skyscrapers and vast slums. As in all cities of the world, in an African city rights belong to the strongest. In modern urban society this seems always to be the case.

FOOTNOTES:

1. Dathorne 1974, 409 ff.
2. Guy Menga 1969.
3. Ibid, pp 66 — 68.
4. 1964.
5. See also Sutherland 1967a.
6. Imbuga (Kenya) 1971.

7. Ibid, p 13.
8. 1967b.
9. Owusu 1973, pp 17, 18.
10. 1973.
11. 1972.
12. 1946.
13. Elebe 1973.
14. 1968.
15. Ngugi.
16. Ibid, p 13.
17. Ibid, pp 63 — 64.
18. 1964.
19. 1965.
20. Easmon 1964, pp 55 — 56.
21. Easmon 1965, p 35.
22. 1964.
23. 1954.
24. Aidoo 1968, Ngugi 1968, De Graft 1970.
25. 1964, 1970, 1971.
26. 1964.
27. Oyono-Mbia 1964, pp 35 — 39.
28. Ibid, p 112.
29. Ibid, p 6.
30. Easmon 1964.
31. Easmon 1965, p 36.
32. cf. De Graft 1964.
33. Imbuga 1973, p 22.
34. 1968, p 11.
35. Nénékhaly-Camara 1970, p 44.
36. See also Pliya 1973.
37. Imbuga 1973, pp 53 — 54.
38. See Mbughuni 1976.
39. Tambueni Haki Zetu 1973.
40. Hatia 1972.
41. 1960.

42. 1964.
43. Njau 1960, pp 13, 14.
44. Menga 1969.

VI. The World of the Big City

The rate of development in Africa in recent decades has not greatly influenced life in most villages. Cities on the other hand have grown tremendously by the influx of people wanting to settle in them. Urban areas are characterised by enormous contrasts. The governments of most African countries try to impress their own people and foreign visitors by the construction of modern buildings without asking themselves whether their people profit from these concrete monsters.

On the other hand there are rapidly growing slums where every inhabitant is hoping to share something of the country's prosperity. This wealth is no longer in the hands of foreigners. Today an African elite is also making large profits.

Living in the city facilitates the finding of employment. Opportunities for office or factory work hardly exist in the villages. In the city community life has a completely different pattern to what it has in the villages. The opportunities for people of different ethnic groups to meet are far more frequent. Under these conditions strains between people of different clans can increase to such an extent that conflicts become unavoidable. Tribal relations often play a part in national politics. It can be vital to have a brother who is a minister or a secretary of state, because such a person can get you a job that you would never have found solely by virtue of your abilities.

In the city ideas concerning family relations, friendship, marriage, morals and clothing change. Young people feel more independent in the anonymity of the big city. They escape more easily from the obligations of the unwritten village rules, and parental authority.

For young people the city has a magical attraction. From afar life seems richer and more exciting there, even if it is only because of the electric lights, the cinemas, the bars and night clubs. In comparison with village life there is much more to experience in the city. For many people the unhappy experiences are more common than the happy ones. There are more possibilities of earning money than in the village, but most travellers to the city realize too late that the number of jobs is limited and that they have hardly any training for the existing opportunities. The struggle for life is hard, corruption is wide-spread and the weak are often trampled on by the strong. In urban areas, as several playwrights have shown, the concern of the individual is to maintain himself in a disrupted society.

BIG AND SMALL PROFITEERS

Rapidly rising politicians, trade union leaders, and businessmen make as much profit from their positions as they can because they know very well that wealth is often a very vulnerable possession. At any moment fate can turn against them. In Easmon's *The New Patriots*[1] minister Byeloh embezzles funds and has to come before a judge.

That power corrupts is also the message of Dadié's *Les voix dans le vent.*[2] In *L'homme qui tua le crocodile*[3] by the Congolese writer Sylvain Bemba it is a rich businessman, N'Gandou, who tyrannizes and exploits the whole area, until a teacher from the local school protests and 'the crocodile' gets what he deserves. In this tragi-comedy an important role is played by the *amuseur public,* who is midway between a traditional narrator, a comic and a town crier. In the area where the rich N'Gandou stays he tells the people the fable of the crocodile that wants the whole river for itself. It is clear whom he is referring to and frequently the audience repeat parts enthusiastically. Those who owe him money have to pay interest on the amount, or otherwise send their wives or daughters to the crocodile. In the end the *amuseur public* says:

> I do not like telling this story, but I am pleased that you have understood it. It is necessary that our area should wake up for a change. But you know the proverb of the old ones: if you wake a sleeper too roughly the spirits are disturbed.[4]

Then the fight against N'Gandou is waged, and the teacher plays the most important role. The *amuseur public* keeps the people informed of developments, and after the death of N'Gandou he exhorts them to remain vigilant, because on any day new N'Gandous may arise to exploit the people . . .

Forms of corruption and the abuse of power are very varied and are often brought to light in the theatre. The fact that women are often forced to render sexual services to find a job or for subsistence is a sad reality in African cities.[5] This is reflected in plays like *L'homme qui tua le crocodile* and Jean Pliya's *La secrétaire particuliere.*[6] John Ruganda's *Black Mamba*[7] is a satire in which Ruganda denounces the abuse of women by men as commercial objects. The English professor, Coarx, does not know that his mistress is the wife of his servant Berewa. Berewa uses his wife in this way so that she can earn something extra. But, after the first time, Namuddu says that she finds it terrible and that she does not wish to continue with this way of making money. She proposes looking for another job, but no work pays as much:

Berewa:	Imagine, dear Namuddu, just last night you made a hundred shillings. I have to work a whole month to get the same amount. My wife, I don't see why you should be so upset by this idea . . .
Namuddu:	But how can I go on sleeping? How can I do it? O God!
Berewa:	Think of something else while you are doing it.
Namuddu:	It is all the same. Supposing he made me pregnant?
Berewa:	No, Namuddu, the professor is not an idiot. Perhaps you don't like the way he

smells, but think of me, think of our
poverty, think of our future riches while
you are busy.

Namuddu: Did you expect me to do this when you
called me to the city?

Berewa: It's just that I knew . . . you would dig
deep into his heart and his pocket too. If
less beautiful women have been able to do
it, why not you, Namuddu? . . . Poverty
hooked us. We must hook riches. That's
the fashion these days. Many families have
become prosperous that way. No reason
why we should not.[8]

It is not only on the stage that some city dwellers
reason this way.[9] Ime Ikiddeh's *Blind Cyclos*[10]
presents similar problems of the city in short scenes.
Every scene — here called a round — is introduced by
a few wise but obscure words from a blind seer. The
seer is the link between the past, the present and
the future. He has the thread of events in his hands.

Akonnedi: I am Akonnedi, the medicine man. My
knowledge comes from the Seven Stars.
Confined to this shrine I move with the
winds. Flit thro' swamps in and out with
tides at sea. Blind I have the habit of sight.
An owl by night, a crow by day. As now
from my hut I well can see Chairman
Olemu beginning his rounds. And, people
of our land, this is Round One.[11]

This 'Chairman', as he is called, is a resourceful
businessman who enriches himself by means of
various corrupt transactions, and then still tries to

overcharge several poor tenants. Elisa is the Chairman's mistress and Samuel is his chauffeur. Elisa has just visited her friend, Nkem.

Elisa: Nkem does not keep his money — he drinks like a gutter. When I arrived he was broke, and I had to give him two pounds.

Samuel: Does Chairman know about him?

Elisa: Chairman thinks I go to Ibadan to see my father. The poor man died four years ago and I had to leave the convent school. But one day Chairman may find out. Oh, I am so worried.

Samuel: That's no problem, Miss. There are many ways of catching a rat. I can take you to a medicine man seven miles from here. He can make proper medicine and close the eyes of both men so that they won't worry . . . The man is the brother of the husband of my wife's sister. I am not telling you a story. I know him. I have taken people there before, bishops, ministers and so on. They all come back to thank me . . . But you will give me a small commission, Miss.

Elisa: I will give you . . . I will come and visit you, Sammy, if your wife does not fight me.

Samuel: We can arrange that . . . There's one thing. The medicine will go deep if Chairman goes there in person.

Elisa: I can manage that. Chairman will go anywhere there's hope of more money, and now he is worried about the elections too. He is ready to do what I tell him provided I have no other man.[12]

In the city everything centres around money, just as used to be the case in the white colonial community. In African literature the whites are often depicted as being there only to improve their material positions. The god of the white man lives in his purse, otherwise he wouldn't write on his money 'In God we trust' or 'God with us'. Among the African elite money plays a similar role. Everyone tries to taste a small piece of the cake of prosperity.

HIGH LIFE AND MISERY

In Africa the idea of high life is pleasure, music, dancing, drinking, free love, pretty clothes and the indiscriminate spending of money. This dream world is mirrored in glamorous western films which are often seen in Africa.

Most city dwellers realise the high life is not for them. In *The Transistor Radio*[13] by the Nigerian, Tsaro-Wiwa, we meet Basi and Alali, two jobless fellows in Lagos, who cannot decide whether to go back to their village, even though they are always hungry in the city and cannot find work anywhere.

Alali: I'm sick of it. Thoroughly sick. The pity is, each time I make up my mind to go away, I find I can't. Something seems to be asking me to stay on.

Basi: I have experienced them all, and more. For three good years, Alali, I roamed this city. I and the streets of Lagos are friends. I know their names. They recognise my footsteps. Three years I was at it, and no help came. Then, one day, and almost unexpected too, it happened. Messenger in an office. I jumped at it. It was worth holding on to. Then the chief clerk got sour. In a week he had sent me three queries. The following week I was out and his relative was in. But I am not complaining.

Alali: It is a shame. Why do they send us to school if they won't give us jobs?

Basi: What can you do with a Class Four Certificate? they ask. What couldn't I do? That's my answer. Why, I could name a hundred people in this town who earn over 1 000 pounds a year, without having seen the gate of a secondary school.[14]

They have a bit of luck when their landlady threatens to put them out of the house because they haven't paid rent for many months. She leaves behind an empty Heineken bottle which she had brought with her. This bottle brings the transistor radio. The radio is a prize in an advertising stunt when by means of the empty bottle they prove that they drink Heineken. The radio also creates problems because of an obligatory listener's licence, but lucky chances like this diminish any likelihood of a return to the slow peaceful rhythm of the village. The nervous vibrancy of cities such as Lagos, Dakar, Kinshasa or Nairobi has its own magic. There is always hope that one day everything will change.

The Burdens[15] by the Ugandan, John Ruganda, shows the return to misery of a cabinet minister who lived in a dream world. After independence Wamala became a minister and was cheered by enthusiastic crowds, but one day he went too far in his thirst for power. Charged with an attempt to arrange a coup with foreign support, he has to go to jail for two years. All his possessions are confiscated. After his release he cannot bear going back to his previous poverty and to the same people that his family had broken with when he was rich. Totally isolated, they live in a poor area. Wamala turns to drink and his wife tries to sustain the family by weaving mats. Reality is cruel and the dream too brief.

Tinka:	The way you held me when the Union Jack was lowered. Do you remember?
Wamala:	Hand-in-hand among the independence crowds on the decorated rostrum. We were big shots then.
Tinka:	Shopping at the supermarket over the phone.
Wamala:	Business deals done at the Intercontinental.
Tinka:	The hairdresser coming home.
Wamala:	Bank managers in my study.
Tinka:	An insidious upsurge of relatives and friends.
Wamala:	You always threw them out.
Tinka:	Where are they now?
Wamala:	The vermin.[16]

There is no stability left. The relatives that were rejected in the past themselves reject the ex-politician. He is now just another slumdweller.

It is clear that the poor in the cities are unable to change their miserable situation. They miss the stability and co-operation of village life. People have to organize themselves if they hope to improve their lot. This is the message of the Ivory Coast's Zadi in *L'oeil*[17] and of Kenya's Ngugi in *This Time Tomorrow*.[18]

The high life of the elite is enjoyed at the cost of the masses for whom independence has brought nothing. In *This Time Tomorrow* the community council has decided to demolish a whole suburb, because slums leave an unfavourable impression with tourists. Their opinions have more weight than the trampled interests of the inhabitants of Uhuru Market, as the suburb is called. Old Njango has lost her husband in the battle for independence and she is now thrown out of her house, which is being destroyed by bulldozers. For her there is no future, but her daughter Wanjiru still has hope for a change in the social climate. She is still young and has listened to the words of the 'Stranger'. According to him the world will belong to the poor farmers and the labourers who had fought for Uhuru.

L'oeil is a symbol in Zadi's short piece. The wife of an enriched politician has lost her eye in a car accident, and she is inconsolable. Her husband decides to buy her a new eye. He offers fifty thousand francs to the man prepared to force his own wife to give her eye for a transplant. Djédjé is in financial difficulties: he is persuaded, and sells the eye of his wife. A short while later she dies, but Djédjé is richly rewarded for his wife and for his devotion to his country. He gets the job of *président-directeur-général* of a business. But the eye is the cause of unrest among students and labourers. They realise that they have been blind and that they have been manipulated by the elite. The eye is a symbol, the writing on the wall. 'For it is important that one should see clearly,' Zadi says in his introduction.[19] Here, as in Sembène Ousmane's novel, *Xala*[20] the poor react against their position. In both cases they have reality forced upon them by troops protecting law and order.

To counteract irregularities the unemployed are sometimes taken back to the villages in trucks and threatened with jail sentences if they dare show themselves in the city without work permits or work. Such measures have little effect. The cities keep on growing. New slums spring up on the edge of the city like mushrooms and the unemployed keep coming to the city like insects being attracted by a candle.

POPULAR THEATRE IN THE CITY

If one speaks of the opposing forces of the rich and the poor, of the masses and the elite, then it is perhaps necessary to ask at whom this theatre, that is written mainly in European languages, is aimed.

It has already been noted that the distinction between literary theatre and popular theatre is becoming more and more marked. On the one hand there are plays being published that have never been performed, while some popular productions have never even been offered to a publisher. A systematic investigation of this phenomenon has not yet been done in Africa. It is obvious that a European publisher would see little profit in a popular play in which different languages are used side by side, and which are only understood by the public of the area for which it has been written. This public is bi- or tri-lingual and the popular playwright exploits this. It gives an extra dimension to his play which will be appreciated by the audience for which it is written. A Christmas play I saw performed in 1965 in Kisangani was in Kiswahili (the local tongue) but the soldiers in it spoke Lihgala (the language of the Zairean army) while the officials spoke French (the language of the administration). In this way different languages can be used to add authenticity to a work. Michael Etherton, who edited a work in two volumes, called *African Plays for Playing*,[21] came to the same conclusion in an article[22] in which he discussed the use by popular dramatists of more than one language in a play. Examples he took were from the work of the Zambian, Kasoma, and the Cameroonian, Musinga.

The writer of the popular play is not only inspired by the life of the ordinary man in the city, but he also writes for that ordinary man and not for the elite. Etherton talks of an *urban pop culture* which has developed in the city, a mixture of traditional and new elements, of which the results are sometimes very original. Unfortunately the official government representatives who have to decide about subsidies seem to lack enthusiasm for this new popular culture. In most independent African countries the so-called authenticity of the ancient tradition, and not western-influenced creativity, is considered to be the norm for artistic value. Traditional dancing groups receive subsidies and are sent to the western world as visiting cards from Africa, even though the dancing is often performed out of context and executed in a western way. Ordinary people do their own dances without considering whether they are western or authentic.

It is for such a public that Kasoma has written. He has discovered how difficult it is for a writer to resist the temptation of writing exclusively for the middle class. He says, 'In Africa the theatre must go to the people, rather than expect the people to come to it.'[24] In *The Long Arms of the Law*[24] Kasoma tells about city life in a popular part of Zambia's Copper-

belt. The pretty Angela threatens her husband
Kapama with a rich city youth called Pumpken.
Kapama realizes that the two of them want to get rid
of him but he acts as if he knows nothing about it.

To illustrate the different levels of language the
text is rendered untranslated. When Angela comes in
she sings a popular English song.

Angela: *(Sings)* Please come back to me, sweetheart.
           I am so sad and lonely.
           I will never do without you . . . *(bis)*
           (Talking) Ho! I am feeling drowsy. Let me go
           to sleep. *(She goes to bed)*

*(Enter Kapama, pretending to be coming home from
work and happily singing a political song)*

Kapama: *(Singing)* Nibani baleteka?
           Owe na Kaunda
           Nibani baleteka?
           Owe ba Kaunda
           Chawama chasokona lelo ba Kaunda
           Abana ba Zambia balefwaya ubuntungwa lelo!
               (bis)
           (Knocks) My darling, Angela. Open the door
           for me. Hey, Angela, are you there? Open the
           door for me.
           (Angela wakes and lights are switched on)
Angela: Oh, Kapama, why are you so late tonight?
           You know I become worried when you
           remain out so late at night. Have you been
           doing overtime again?
Kapama: That's right, my dear! I have been doing
           overtime to earn enough to enable me to buy
           that Humber bicycle I spoke of the other day.

Do you remember, dear?[25]

The songs have a meaning of their own in the local
context. Angela is singing in English because by her
relationship with Pumpken she has found new status.
Kapama is singing in Bemba. The Humber cycle is the
highest symbol of prosperity with which Kapama can
present his wife. At the same time Angela is being
taken out in a motor car by her lover. In Pumpken's
letter that Kapama intercepts by chance, he says that
money is no problem 'to some of us.'[26] To obtain his
car Pumpken obviously did not work overtime. In his
article[27] Etherton gives interesting examples of the
use of more than one language in Kasoma's plays.

This Zambian author continually alludes to local
situations, political leaders and events of which
everyone is aware. The public feels closely involved
with events on stage and reacts with enthusiasm.

Etherton compares the plays of popular writers
like Kasoma[28] and Musinga[29] with the Ghanaian
Concert Parties[30] and the Nigerian folk opera or
Sentogo's theatre in Uganda.[31] Alain Ricard[32]
describes how in Togo, the distinction is made
between *théatre scolaire* and *théatre populaire*. In
Togo, popular theatre in the city is called *concert*, as
it is in Ghana. Similar tendencies are also found in
South African theatre groups in African townships.
Some groups were founded by SASO, the black
student movement. Such groups were part of an
explosion of cultural activities, most often working
without texts in order to avoid censorship. Examples
of published South African plays, based on the
situation in the African townships, are found in the
work of Leshoai.[33] His work is published in East
Africa. Mqayisa's *Confused Mhlaba*[34] was published

in South Africa, but was banned after a number of performances. The play is about the return of an ex-Robben Island prisoner and his attempts to adapt to normal life in a black township.

Most of this popular theatre originates from a mixture of western and African elements that arises out of the social conflicts in the big African cities. The main theme is almost always the search for material security and human contact in the hard reality of urbanized society. The result can be original and whether it is published or not, is applauded by the people about whom it is written and for whom it is intended.

FOOTNOTES:

1. 1965.
2. 1970.
3. 1972.
4. Bemba 1972, p 71.
5. Little 1973.
6. 1972.
7. 1973.
8. Ruganda 1973, pp 11, 12.
9. Little 1973.
10. 1970.
11. Ikiddeh 1970, p 111.
12. Ibid, p 115.
13. 1973.
14. Tsaro-Wiwa 1973, pp 90, 91.
15. 1972.
16. Ruganda 1972, p 41, 42.

17. 1975.
18. 1973.
19. 1975, p 168.
20. 1973.
21. 1974a and 1975b.
22. 1976.
23. Quoted by Etherton 1975a, p 5.
24. 1968.
25. Kasoma 1968.
26. Ibid, p 19.
27. 1976, pp 30 — 36.
28. 1968, 1973, 1975.
29. 1975.
30. De Graft 1976, pp 14 ff.
31. Sentogo 1975.
32. 1975.
33. 1972, see also the Ravan playscript series.
34. 1970.

VII. Theatre and Society: the Vision of Wole Soyinka

The artist has always functioned in African society as the record of the mores and experience of his society *and* as the voice of vision in his own time.

Wole Soyinka

Wole Soyinka is a leading writer in Nigeria, his own country, as well as in the rest of Africa, Europe and America. Into his work he has integrated most facets of the African experience. Between the poles of tradition and change he searches for essential human values, which he tries to make universally recognisable from an African perspective. Because he has most convincingly succeeded, and because interest in his work is growing throughout the world, it seems logical to give special attention to this playwright.

Soyinka was born in 1934 in Abeoluta, Nigeria. He studied English in Ibadan and Leeds and from 1958 to 1960 was attached to the Royal Court Theatre in London. During this time he wrote his first successful plays, the *Swamp Dwellers*[1] and *The Lion and the*

Jewel.[2] In 1960 he returned to Nigeria with a scholarship to study traditional African forms of theatre. This bursary gave him the opportunity to travel throughout Nigeria and study traditional festivals, rituals and masquerades. This influence became clear in his own plays. He was a lecturer at the university of Ibadan, where he started a theatre group and later was appointed director of the School of Drama.

Soyinka was arrested in October 1965 on suspicion of smuggling an Action group tape onto the turntable at Radio Ibadan. Shortly before the broadcast, a tape with a speech by the regional Prime Minister was replaced. The country heard 'the voice of the opposition' requesting the Premier to retire. Because of lack of evidence he was released, but in 1967 he was arrested again and sentenced to more than two years' imprisonment on a charge of anti-government activities during the Nigerian civil war. After almost two years of solitary confinement he was released in October 1969. His experiences are recorded in his prison notes entitled *The Man Died.*[3] For a while he lived in Accra in self-imposed exile, but returned to his own country in December 1975, where he is now head of the department of dramatic arts at the University of Ife.

So far Soyinka has published more than ten plays. He is also a poet, novelist, essayist, critic, translator, actor, director, lecturer and publisher. It is clear that one cannot discuss his work in a few pages, and several books and many articles on his work have already been published.[4]

BACKGROUNDS AND INFLUENCES

Soyinka's deep roots in Yoruba culture can be seen in all his work. Gods, spirits, powers and ancestors are presented, while traditional music, songs and dances also have a function in his plays.

Yet the African tradition is not his only source. He also uses ideas from western culture. Through his study in England, his many travels and his work at the Royal Court Theatre, he made contact with the most divergent forms of theatre, from classical to *avant garde*. In his work English critics have discovered influence from, among others, Ibsen, Chekov, Wesker and Pinter. Christian motifs are also discernible. In one interview, cited by Jones,[5] Soyinka says that he is no longer a practising Christian, but the influence of his Christian education is evident in biblical images, themes and allusions. A biblical influence is clear in poems from *Idanre and Other Poems*[6] and *A Shuttle in the Crypt,*[7] his novel *The Interpreters*[8] and different plays. Eman in *The Strong Breed*[9] reminds one of Christ, both taking upon themselves the guilt of mankind.

The prophet, Brother Jero,[10] appears in two satirical comedies. In *The Road*[11] the Professor searches old newspapers for the Word, while Christianity is parodied in *Madmen and Specialists.*[12] Soyinka seems to have a love-hate relationship with Christianity.[13] Occasionally it emerges in his work alongside the almost constant Yoruba influence.

In his plays very different experiences are unified in an original way. His view of the world has been widened through his travels and his contact with other cultures, but in the first place he remains an African writer who situates his work in an African context and who writes primarily for an African public.

TRADITIONAL ELEMENTS

There is a marked use in his plays of traditional African, mostly Yoruba sayings and expressions, songs, dances and festivals. For instance, in *A Dance of the Forest*[14] Aboreko the 'elder of the sealed lips' says to another notable:

> The eye that looks downwards will certainly see the nose. The hand that dips to the bottom of the pot will eat the biggest snail. The sky grows no grass but if the earth called her barren, it will drink no more milk. The foot of the snake is not split in two like a man's or in hundreds like the centipede's, but if Agere could dance patiently like the snake, he will uncoil the chain that leads into death . . . [15]

Such current expressions all come from his Yoruba background. Often they do not only have a meaning within the direct context, but contain a more universal wisdom that is relevant to other times and places.[16]

The songs can be divided into two kinds. There are traditional songs to which the author has added a personal note, and there are also songs that have been made popular by recordings and the radio and which in their own way became part of developing traditional genres.[17]

In *Death and the King's Horseman* the horseman of king Elesin performs a dance to the accompaniment of a drum as he sings the story of the Not-I bird.

Death came calling.
Who does not know his rasp of reeds?
A twilight whisper in the leaves before
The great araba falls? Did you hear it?
'Not I,' swears the farmer. He snaps
His fingers around his head, abandons
A hard-worn harvest and begins
A rapid dialogue with his legs.

'Not I,' shouts the fearless hunter, 'but
It's getting dark, and this night-lamp
Has leaked out all its oil. I think
It's best to go home and resume my hunt
Another day.' But now he pauses, suddenly
Letting out a wail. 'Oh foolish mouth, calling
Down a curse on your own head! Your lamp
Has leaked out all its oil, has it?'
Forwards or backwards now he dare not move.[18]

People and animals fear the Not-I bird, Elesin narrates
in song and mime. According to the old custom that
the king's horseman has to accompany the king,
Elesin has to die soon. One of the by-standers asks
how he feels about death.

I, when that Not-I bird perched
Upon my roof, bade him seek his nest again.
Safe, without care or fear I unrolled
My welcome mat for him to see. Not-I
Flew happily away. You'll hear his voice
No more in this lifetime — You all know
What I am . . .

My rein is loosened,
I am master of my Fate. When the hour comes

> Watch me dance along the narrowing path
> Glazed by the soles of my great precursors.
> My soul is eager, I shall not turn aside.

One example of the use of a popular Nigerian song from the fifties, can be found in *The Road*,[19] where one of the characters sings in Yoruba, while others join in:

> It's a long long road to heaven
> It's a long long road to heaven, Driver
> Go easy a-ah go easy, Driver.
> It's a long long road to heaven.
> My Creator, be not harsh with me.

Soyinka talks of a *driver's dirge*. The song underlines the theme of the play that death lies waiting on the road. Soyinka was inspired by the road between Ibadan and Lagos on which road users are constantly in danger.

Another example can be found in *Madmen and Specialists*[20] where the beggars sing a variation on *When the Saints*. In this play they represent the suppressed within a totalitarian system which tries to profit by serving as agents of the Intelligence Service. The beggars function as the choir within the play's structure.[21]

Another important element in Soyinka's plays is the festival.[22] Festivals are very popular in Nigeria. Originally they had a religious meaning, but more dramatic forms developed as the meaning of the ritual was gradually lost. They are open-air performances where the occasion is often used to criticize certain social or political evils. Critical questions are asked and songs sung in which the audience enthusiastically participates.

A festival has a special atmosphere. The preparations alone create a scene of excitements. The pre-festival tension is almost tangible in some of Soyinka's plays. In *Kongi's Harvest*[23] the theme is the symbolism of the New Yam, the ancient life-giving spirit, the sign of fertility and of the tilling of the soil.[24]

Kongi represents the modern dictator who abuses the people's respect for old rituals and exploits tradition to enhance his own power. When the great day breaks and Kongi is to be given the first of the New Yams it appears that, despite amnesty rules, Kongi intends to hang several political opponents on the day of the festival. One of them is shot while making an attempt on the life of the dictator. The daughter of the victim, who is herself a member of the resistance, sees to it that at the last moment the head of her father, hidden in a copper pot, is given to Kongi instead of the First Yam. When the lid is removed the bystanders see the head of the old man and everyone flees in panic. Only Kongi remains, paralysed by fear, staring at the gift. The end of the festival illustrates the conflict between the harvest feast of life, as his subjects wish to celebrate it, and the real harvest of an administration in which human lives are not important. *Kongi's Harvest* leaves few illusions about totalitarian governments. Only the resistance symbolizes a gleam of hope. Soyinka's debt to the Bible story of John the Baptist is obvious.

AFRICAN HERITAGE AND NEGRITUDE

Soyinka's work is filled with ideas from his African

cultural heritage. He stands close to the 'return to the sources' to which Senghor refers in his negritude philosophy.[25] According to the Senegalese poet *negritude* is the basis of the cultural heritage, values and spirit of African civilization. The negritude movement originated in reaction to colonial cultural domination.

Senghor thinks that the colonizer justified the political, economic and cultural dependence of the African with the *tabula rasa* theory:

> According to him we have invented nothing, created nothing in the artistic world, sculptured nothing, painted nothing and made no music. To attain a meaningful change we had to get rid of our borrowed clothes, the clothes of assimilation.[26]

Soyinka kept a distance between himself and the negritude writers, especially the French African writers. In his now famous dictum he is as little concerned with meditating on his Africanness or his negritude as the tiger has the need to talk about his 'tigritude'. In a discussion with American students at the University of Washington he explained his point of view. He said that negritude was the cause of a group of alienated people who had practically no contact with their own culture: Negritude is part of a European philosophy, which explains why intellectuals like Sartre were enthusiastic about it. Essentially its concern is to place the African personality within a European frame of reference.[27]

Another difference from Senghor and his supporters is that Soyinka does not idealise 'mother Africa', as Jones[28] has rightly noted. To Soyinka the forefathers were no better than the present generation. Like us they were capable of performing great deeds, and yet no less acts of folly and egoism. Also the gods were guilty of callousness and caprice in their relationships with people. They are also therefore to be judged.

A similar accusation is made against men and gods in *A Dance of the Forests*[29] which was performed for the first time at Nigeria's independence festivities. Here also there is no space for idealizing. No miracles can be expected from independence, just as the past has been no paradise. Negritude literature wants the world to believe in an idealized Africa, according to Wole Soyinka.

SCEPTICAL QUESTIONS

Soyinka is a sceptic who disturbs the audience with questions like those asked in *The Swamp Dwellers*. The play concerns a village which lies isolated in a marshy area (The Niger delta?) and is influenced only to a small degree by the outside world. The young people are leaving for the city and the swamp is becoming a threat to the survival of the village, the symbol of society. The Snake of the Swamp is the divinity which has to be placated. Only Kadiye, the priest, can prevent the swallowing of the meagre crop by the greedy water. The action takes place in a poor hut in the marsh village, where an old couple are waiting for the return of their son, Igwezu. The young man has gone out to take stock of the damage done to the lands by the Snake. Igwezu is an embittered person. His brother in the city has stolen his money and his wife, and his crop is again destroyed. He has returned from the city without illusions and it is obvious that he is not expecting anything from his village and his lands. All his venom is turned against Kadiye when he comes in to be shaved (Igwezu and his father are the barbers of the village). While shaving the priest he questions him. Does he not speak with the 'voice of the gods'?

Igwezu: Who must appease the Serpent of the Swamp?

Kadiye: The Kadiye.

Igwezu: Who takes the gifts of the people, in order that the beast may be gorged and made sleepy-eyed with the feast of sacrifice?

Kadiye: The Kadiye.

Igwezu: *(His speech is increasing in speed and intensity.)* On whom does the land depend for the benevolence of the reptile? Tell me that, priest. Answer in one word.

Kadiye: Kadiye.

Igwezu: Do I not offer my goats to the priest?

Kadiye: Yes.

Igwezu: And did he offer them in turn to the serpent?

Kadiye: He did.

Igwezu: Everything which he received from the grain to the bull?

Kadiye: Everything.

Igwezu: The goat and the white cockerel which I gave before I left?

Kadiye: Every hair and feather on them . . .

Igwezu: And ever since I began to till the soil, did I not give the soil his due? Did I not bring the first of the lentils to the shrine, and put the first oil upon the altar?

Kadiye: Regularly.

Igwezu: And when the Kadiye blessed my marriage, and tied the heaven-made knot, did he not

                promise a long life? Did he not promise
                children? Did he not promise happiness?
                ... Why are you so fat, Kadiye?

Makuri: May heaven forgive what has been uttered
                here tonight. May earth reject the folly
                spoken by my son.

Igwezu: You lie upon the land, Kadiye, and choke it in
                the folds of a serpent.

Makuri: Son, listen to me ...

Igwezu: If I slew the fatted calf, Kadiye, do you think
                the land might breathe again? If I slew all the
                cattle in the land and sacrificed every measure
                of goodness, would it make any difference to
                our fates?[30]

From Igwezu's questions it is obvious that he dis-
trusts ancient ideas. That which the older people
accept as inevitable, the younger people are gradually
seeing in a different light. It is not necessarily true
that fate is determined by the caprice of the gods.
But Igwezu did not have many pleasant experiences
in the city either. Soyinka offers no easy solutions.
Only personal responsibility and the will of man can
change society.

TRADITION OR PROGRESS?

It would be wrong to conclude from Soyinka's work
that he favours tradition above progress. In *The Lion
and the Jewel* the girl, Sidi, prefers the much older
and polygamous Bale (the chief) to the young,
'modern' school teacher, Lakunle. However, the
theme of this play is not the contrast between
tradition and progress, but that between truth and

falsehood.[31] Lakunle has only superficial ideas about development and progress, as is clear in his proposal to Sidi.

Lakunle: When we are wed, you shall not walk or sit
       Tethered, as it were, to my dirtied heels.
       Together we shall sit at table,
       Not on the floor, and eat,
       Not with fingers, but with knives
       And forks, and breakable plates
       Like civilized beings.
       I will not have you wait on me
       Till I have dined my fill.
       No wife of mine, no lawful wedded wife
       Shall eat the leavings off my plate.
       That is for children.
       I want to walk beside you in the street,
       Side by side and arm in arm
       Just like the Lagos couples I have seen.
       High-heeled shoes for the lady, red paint
       On her lips. And her hair is stretched
       Like a magazine photo. I will teach you
       The waltz and we'll both learn the foxtrot
       And we'll spend the week-end in night-clubs at Ibadan.
       Oh I must show you the grandeur of towns.
       We'll live there if you like or merely pay visits.
       So choose. Be a modern wife, look me in the eye
       And give me a little kiss — like this.
       (Kisses her.)
Sidi: No, don't! I tell you I dislike
       This strange unhealthy mouthing you perform.[32]

The Bale explains to Sidi that he is not against progress, but that the consequences should not be underestimated. According to him uniformity is a fatal result of progress: all the roofs and faces are beginning to look the same. There are also murderous roads exacting many victims. The Bale is a wise man who considers the pros and cons before he concedes to change, while Lakunle is an immature youth with a little overworked knowledge from books.

Also in *Death and the King's Horseman* tradition is opposed to a western idea of change. The story takes place during colonial times against the background of the Second World War and is partially based on fact. Olunde, the son of Elesin the king's horseman, returns from England in expectation of the death of his father, who through his own will-power and concentration is going to die now that the king is dead. Olunde has seen what war in the West is. Despite bloody battles with numerous victims they still speak triumphantly of success. His conclusion is that the English have no right to judge other nations and their customs. The function of the king's horseman is passed from generation to generation in the family. Elesin has known from his youth that he as the eldest son will have to die to accompany the king on his last journey. Before Elesin has to die the colonial district officer intervenes. To him this seems like a barbaric human sacrifice, a view he obviously does not have about western world wars, which are barbaric in the eyes of Africans. They also find it insulting that Pilkings and his wife clothe themselves in traditional Egungun costumes and masks for a banal fancy dress. The district officer does not realize that he is guilty of sacrilege in the eyes of the adherents of this traditional religion.

The intervention of Pilkings has tragic consequences. He believes that he has saved Elesin by putting him behind bars. A procession of mourning women comes to the prison, carrying on their shoulders a pack rolled into a mat. Sternly Pilkings asks about the purpose of their visit and the contents of the pack. Iyaloja, the mother of the market and the leader of the women, rolls out the mat before him. In it lies the body of Olunde. The boy has taken over the task of his father. From behind the bars Elesin sees the result of his own failing and he commits suicide by throttling himself with the chain of his handcuffs. Pilkings tries to save him by artificial respiration.

Iyaloja: Why do you strain yourself? Why do you labour at tasks for which no one, not even the man lying there would give you thanks? He is gone at last into the passage but oh, how late it all is. His son will feast on the meat and throw him bones. The passage is clogged with droppings from the King's stallion. He will arrive all stained in dung.

Pilkings: *(In a tired voice)* Was this what you wanted?

Iyaloja: No child, it is what you brought to me, you who play with strangers' lives, who even usurp the vestments of our dead, yet believe that the stain of death will not cling to you. The gods demanded only the old expired plantain but you cut down the sap-laden shoot to feed your pride. There is your plate, filled to overflowing. Feast on it.[33]

Here also the theme is not the choice between traditional and western values, but the exposing of false values, which are often as a matter of course adopted by a community, whether the community be traditional or modern.

In theatre as a social phenomenon the relationship between the public and the action is Soyinka's main concern. Although in principle every work of art that enlarges the horizon of the human spirit already can be an instrument of change, he believes that theatre is the most revolutionary form of art. According to him revolution in Africa should mean

> . . . a complete re-examination of principles which we have taken for granted for a very long time: the principle of dependence on outside countries, on the former colonial masters, the principle of the division of Africa into entities some of which are French oriented others which are British oriented, others American in a far more subtle way in spite of America's claims that it has no colonies in Africa . . . [34]

Social values have to be re-defined and freed from outside intervention. 'If every compatriot is not freed from existing exploitation, the ideology of the ruling group has no meaning' were his words in a lecture entitled *The Road from Amilcar Cabral*[35] which he gave to students in Ibadan immediately after his return from exile.

Wole Soyinka is a sceptic who mistrusts power, because power corrupts. According to him the writer ought to occupy himself with the reality of his own society, and fight for the awakening of conscience and for freedom of expression. Soyinka makes this task his own in his life as well as in his work.

FOOTNOTES:

1. 1963.
2. 1963.
3. 1972.
4. e.g. Moore 1971, Jones 1973.
5. 1973
6. 1967.
7. 1972.
8. 1965.
9. 1963.
10. 1963, 1973.
11. 1965.
12. 1971.
13. Berry 1972.
14. 1963.
15. Ibid, p 39.
16. Ogumba 1970a, pp 3 — 5.
17. Ibid, 5 ff.
18. 1975, pp 11, 12.
19. 1965, p 19.
20. 1971, p 60.
21. 1975a, p 119.
22. *The Strong Breed* 1963, *A Dance of the Forests,* 1963, *The Road,* 1965, *Kongi's Harvest,* 1967.
23. 1967.
24. Ogumba 1970a, p 11.
25. 1964b.
26. Kesteloot 1963, p 110.
27. Soyinka 1975a, pp 101, 102.
28. 1971a, p 114.
29. 1963.
30. 1963, pp 37 — 39.
31. Jones 1971a, p 117, 1971b, p 130.
32. 1963, pp 9, 10.

33. 1975, p 76.
34. 1975a, pp 65, 128.
35. 1975b.

VIII. Conclusion

Ritual is certainly one of the origins of the theatre and in the best dramatic forms something of the ritual character always remains. Soyinka explains the success of Albee's *Who's Afraid of Virginia Woolf?* in Cuba from the fact that the author 'exploited a recognizable ritual of purgation'.[1]

Since ancient times in African theatre the whole community has been involved. This is a total theatre where music, dancing and mime take an important place next to the spoken word.

According to Joe de Graft[2] one should really make a distinction between what he calls *magical theatre*, where the actor gradually becomes 'possessed' during the ritual by the character he portrays, and *dramatic art*, where the actor has intellectual and emotional control of the part he is playing. Certain Nigerian masquerades and Haitian voodoo rites[3] are good examples of magical theatre. It is difficult, however, to separate the two areas clearly. Sometimes the masquerade is purely a religious affair. The Egungun

masks are the personification of the ancestors and
touching them may cause death, while the Agbegijo
group of the same Egungun society is not part of the
cult and are concerned with providing popular amuse-
ment.[4] Often the forms are mixed. In contemporary
African theatre various genres co-exist:

Oral literature is still very important. Traditional
theatrical forms, like traditional society itself, is
subject to change. This has always been the case, but
in our time society changes more quickly. In recent
years certain governments have been sponsoring
tribal performances for export. These entertain-
ments are only partly based on the living tradition
and are to a great extent influenced by the demand
for the exotic in terms of western tourist needs. In
the South African context such black dance-dramas
(one thinks of the European tours of *Ipi Tombi* or
Kwa-Zulu) are even more misleading, because, under
white direction, they are presented in the West as a
primitive visiting-card of African culture in South
Africa.

The so-called modern African theatre has not been
completely severed from the oral tradition, but is to a
certain extent a continuation of the older form. It
has, however, in several respects also been influenced
by western theatre:

(1) The language is in most cases European, al-
     though there has been an increase in recent years
     in acting and writing in African languages.
(2) The verbal element is more important than the

music, singing or dancing.

(3) The distance between the audience and the stage has increased and an elevated stage is being used. The curtain underlines the new distance between performer and audience.

(4) The play is presented in a more concentrated form and in a much shorter time than in most traditional performances.

(5) Depending on the society, themes have changed.

(6) Modern performances, especially if given in a hall, are mostly visited by a small upper class of the population.

(7) It is also a characteristic of this theatre that plays are published in book form by European publishers.

Some young playwrights are beginning to realize that a large public exists outside the small circle of spectators from schools and universities. The previously mentioned *popular theatre* in the city is one of the forms developing out of this realization. This development, apart from the use of local language, music and dancing, signifies a continuation of tradition, because the playwright is again working with the intention of addressing the larger public. In this type of theatre there are often political elements. We have already mentioned the activities in the townships of SASO, the South African black student movement. Etherton[5] gives examples of *drama-workshops* as they are organised by students in Zambia, Tanzania, Uganda or Nigeria, where the students work together with ordinary people in the villages or in the suburbs of big cities, labourers in factories or school children.

It should have become obvious that theatre in

Africa has in general been rather distant from the idea of *l'art-pour-l'art*. This is also true of modern theatre in spite of the strong western influence. Music and dancing still play a bigger part in it than in the western theatre, and there is still the inclination towards audience participation.

In Europe and the United States many experiments have been tried to establish a closer relationship between performers and audience, and also between theatre and society. In its search for new forms of dramatic expression western theatre might profitably look outside the walls of its own culture and tradition, and learn from the varied theatrical forms and their social functions in Africa.

FOOTNOTES:

1. 1975a.
2. 1976, 5 ff.
3. Métraux 1959.
4. Beier 1967, p 244.
5. 1975a, p 5.

Bibliography

I AFRICAN LITERARY TEXTS

Aidoo, Christina Ama Ata, 1965, *The dilemma of a ghost*, a play, London, Longman.

Aidoo, Ama Ata, 1970, *Anowa*, a play, London, Longman.

Alkaly, Kaba, 1972, *Nègres, qu'avez-vous fait? Tragédie en trois actes*, Bamako, Editions populaires.

Amale, Samson O.O., 1972, *The leaders*, a play, Ibadan, University of Ibadan, Institute of African Studies, Occasional publication 39.

Badian, Seydou, 1962, *La mort de Chaka*, théâtre, Paris, Présence Africaine.

Basset, René, 1883, *Contes populaires d'Afrique*, Paris, Guilmoto.

Beier, Ulli, 1966, 1971, *African poetry. An anthology of traditional African poems*, Cambridge University Press.

Bemba, Sylvian, 1972, *L'homme qui tua le crocodile*, Yaoundé, CLE, collection théâtre.

Biebuyck, Daniel, 1971, 'The Mwindo Epic', in *The horizon history of Africa* ch VII, Inner Africa, New York, American Heritage Publishing Co. Inc.

Boelaert, E., 1957, *Lianja-verhalen. I. Ekofo-versie*, AMRCB — L,19.

Carey, Margaret, 1970, *Myths and legends of Africa*, London, Hamlyn.

Clark, J.P., 1964, *Three plays, Song of a goat. The masquerade. The raft*, London, Oxford University Press.

Clark, J.P., 1966, *Ozidi*, a play, London/Ibadan, Oxford University Press.

Cook, David, and Lee, Miles (Eds.), (1968) 1972, *Short East African plays in English*, London, Heinemann.

Dadié, Bernard, 1956, *Climbié*, Paris, Seghers.

Dadié, Bernard, 1966, *Légendes et poémes*, Paris, Seghers.

Dadié, Bernard, 1970, *Béatrice du Congo*, théâtre, Paris, Présence Africaine.

Dadié, Bernard, 1970, *Monsieur Thôgô-gnini*, théâtre, Paris, Présence Africaine.

Dadié, Bernard, 1970, *Les voix dans le vent*, Yaoundé, CLE, collection théâtre.

Dervain, Eugéne, 1968, *La reine scélérate suivi de la langue et le scorpion*, Yaoundé, CLE, collection théâtre.

Dia, Amadou Cissé, 1965, *Les derniers jours de Lat Dior, La mort du Damel*, théâtre, Paris, Présence Africaine.

Diop, Birago, (1947) 1965, *Les contes d'Amadou Koumba*, Paris, Présence Africaine.

Diop, Birago, (1958) 1962, *Les nouveaux contes d'Amadou Koumba*, Paris, Présence Africaine.

Diop, Birago, 1960, *Leurres et lueurs*, poémes, Paris, Présence Africaine.

Diop, Birago, 1963, *Contes et lavanes*, Paris, Présence Africaine.

Easmon, R. Sarif, 1964, *Dear parent and ogre*, a play, London, Oxford University Press.

Easmon, R. Sarif, 1965, *The new patriots*, a play, London, Longman.

Elebe, Philippe, 1972, *Simon Kimbangu ou le messie noir*,

(drama en cinq actes) et *Le sang des Noirs pour un sou* (piéce en deux actes et huit tableaux), Paris, Nouvelles Editions Debresse.

Elebe, Lisembe, 1973, *Chant de la terre, chant de l'eau* (adaptation théâtrale du roman Gouverneurs de la rosée de Jacques Roumain), Paris, Oswald collection théâtre.

Eno-Belinga, 1967, 'La jeune fille et l'Emômôtô', in *Anthologie négro-africaine, Panorama critique des prosateurs, poétes et dramaturges noirs du XXe siécle*, sous la rédaction de L. Kestes Loot Verviers, Marabout.

Etherton, Michael (Ed.), 1975a, *African plays for playing, Vol. I*, plays by Hevi, Ajibada and Sentongo, London, Heinemann.

Etherton, Michael (Ed.), 1975b, *African plays for playing, Vol. II*, plays by Kasoma, Musinga and Udensi, London, Heinemann.

Fodeba, Keita, 1965, *Aube Africaine*, Paris, Seghers.

Graft, J.C. de, 1970, *Sons and daughters*, a play, London, Oxford University Press.

Graft, J.C. de, 1970, *Through a film darkly*, a play, London, Oxford University Press.

Hama, Boubou, 1968, *Kotia Nima, I, II, III*, Paris, Présence Africaine.

Henderson, Gwyneth (Ed.), 1973, *African theatre*, eight prize-winning plays chosen by Wole Soyinka, Martin Esslin and Lewis Nkosi, London, Heinemann.

Henderson, Gwyneth and Pieterse, Cosmo (Eds.), 1973, *Nine African plays for radio* London, Heinemann.

Henshaw, Ene, 1974, *This is our chance*, a play, London, University of London Press.

Hussein, Ebrahim N., 1970, *Kinjeketile*, a play, Dar es Salaam, Oxford University Press.

Ijimere, Obotunde, 1966, *The imprisonment of Obatala and other plays*, London, Heinemann.

Ijimerè, Obotunde, (1967), 1969, 'Born with fire on his head', in *Three Nigerian plays* (Introduction and notes Ulli Beier), London, Longman.

Ikiddeh, Ime, (1968) 1970, 'Blind cyclos', in *Ten One-Act plays*, Cosmo Pieterse (Ed.), London, Heinemann.

Imbuga, F.P., 1973, *The married bachelor*, a play, Nairobi, East African Publishing House.

Kâ, Abdou Anta, 1972, *La fille des dieux, Les Amazoulous, Pinthioum Fann, Gouverneurs de la rosée*, théâtre, Paris, Présence Africaine.

Kane, Cheikh Hamidou, 1961, *L'aventure ambigue*, récit, Paris, Julliard.

Kasoma, Kabwe, 1973, *Black Mamba plays*, Lusaka, Neczam.

Kasoma, Kabwe, (1968) 1975, *Black Mamba*, in *African plays for playing*, II, Michael Etherton (Ed.), London, Heinemann.

Kasoma, Kabwe, 1975, 'The long arms of the law', in *The Jewel of Africa, 1, 2, 3*, (in serial form), Lusaka.

Kayor, Franz, 1971, *Les dieux trancheront*, Paris, Oswald collection théâtre.

Knappert, Jan (Ed.), 1971, *Myths and legends of the Congo*, London, Heinemann.

Ladipo, Duro, 1964, *Three Yoruba plays*, Ibadan, Mbari Publications.

Ladipo, Duro, 1967, *Oba Waja*, (English adaptation Ulli Beier), in *Présence Africaine 62(2)*: 148-167.

Ladipo, Duro, (1967) 1969, 'Moremi', in *Three Nigerian plays*, (Introduction and notes Ulli Beier), London, Longman.

Leshoai, B.L., 1972, *The Rendezvous; Revolution; Wrath of the ancestors*, plays, Nairobi, East African Publishing House.

Masiye, A.S., 1973, *The lands of Kazembe*, a play, Lusaka, Neczam.

Mba, Evina Jean, 1974, *Politicos*, Yaoundé, CLE, collection théâtre.

Menga, Guy, 1969, *La marmite de Koka-Mbala*, théâtre, Paris, ORTF-DAEC.

Menga, Guy, 1974, *Les indiscrétions du vagebond*, contes et récits du Congo, Sherbrooke, Eds. Naaman.

Mofolo, Thomas, (1925) 1931, *Chaka, an historical romance*, (English translation from Se-Sotho by F.H. Dutton), London, Oxford University Press.

Mqayisa, Khayalethu, 1974, *Confused Mhlaba*, a play in nine scenes, Johannesburg, Ravan Press.

Muhando, Peninah, 1972, *Hatia* (Guilt), a play, Dar es Salaam, Tanzania Publishing House.

Muhando, Peninah, 1973, *Tambueni haki zetu* (Recognize our rights), a play, Dar es Salaam, Tanzania Publishing House.

Mukasa-Balikuddembe, Joseph, 1972, 'The mirror' in *Short East African plays*, David Cook and Miles Lee (Eds.), London, Heinemann.

Mushiete, Paul and Mikanza, Norbert, 1969, *Pas de feu pur les antilopes*, Kinshasa, Editions Congolia.

Musinga, Victor Eleame, 1975, 'The tragedy of Mr No-Balance', in *African plays for playing*, Michael Etherton (Ed.), London, Heinemann.

Naigiziki, J. Saverio, 1954, *L'optimiste*, piéce de théâtre, Astrida, Groupe scolaire.

Ndao, Cheik A., 1967, *L'exil d'Alboury suivi de La décision*, Paris, Oswald, collection théâtre.

Ndao, Cheik A., 1973, *Le fils de l'Almamy suivi de La case de l'homme*, Paris, Oswald, collection théâtre.

Nenekhaly-Camara, Condetto, 1970, *Continent-Afrique suivi de Amazoulou*, Préface de Mario De Andrade, Paris, Oswald, collection théâtre.

Ngugi wa Thiong'o (James Ngugi), 1968, *The black hermit*, a play, London, Heinemann.

Ngugi wa Thiong'o, 1973, *This time tomorrow*, three plays: 'The rebels'; 'The wound in the heart'; 'This time tomorrow', Nairobi, East African Literature Bureau.

Niane, Djibril Tamsir, 1961, *Soundjata ou l'épopée mandigue*, Paris, Présence Africaine.

Niane, Djibril Tamsir, 1971, *Sikasso ou la derniére citadelle suivi de Chaka,* Préface de Ray Autra, Paris, Oswald, collection théâtre.

Njau, Rebecca, 1960, *The scar,* a play, Nairobi, Kibo Art Gallery.

Njau, Rebecca, 1964, *In the round chain,* a play (mimeograph).

Nkosi, Lewis, 1964, *The rhythm of violence,* a play, London, Oxford University Press.

Nokan, Charles, 1962, *Le soleil noir point,* Paris, Présence Africaine.

Nokan, Charles, 1968, *Abraha Pokou ou une grande Africaine,* Paris, Oswald, collection théâtre.

Nokan, Zégoua (Charles), 1972, *La traversée de la nuit dense suivi de Cris rouges,* Paris, Oswald, collection théâtre.

Obama, Jean-Baptiste, 1972, *Assimilados,* théâtre, Paris, ORTF-DAEC.

Ogunyemi, Wale, (1967) 1969, 'The scheme' in *Three Nigerian Plays* (Introduction and notes, Ulli Beier), London, Longman.

Ogunyemi, Wale, 1972, *Obalúayé,* a Yoruba music-drama, University of Ibadan, Institute of African Studies.

Ogunyemi, Wale, 1973, 'Sign of the rainbow', in *African theatre,* Gwyneth Henderson (Ed.), London, Heinemann.

Omara, Tom, 1972, 'The Exodus', in *Short East African Plays in English,* David Cook and Miles Lee (Eds.), London, Heinemann.

Ousmane, Sembène, 1973, *Xala,* Roman, Présence Africaine.

Owusu, Martin, 1973, *The sudden return and other plays,* London, Heinemann.

Oyono-Mbia, Guillaume, 1969, *Trois prétendants . . . un mari,* Yaoundé, CLE, collection théâtre.

Oyono-Mbia, Guillaume, 1970, *Jusqu'á nouvel avis,* Yaoundé, CLE, collection théâtre.

Oyono-Mbia, Guillaume, 1971, *Notre fille ne se mariera pas,* Paris, ORT-DAEC.

p'Bitek, Okot, 1974, *Horn of my love*, Acoli poetry of Northern Uganda, London, Heinemann.

Pieterse, Cosmo (Ed.), 1972, *Short African plays*, London, Heinemann.

Pieterse, Cosmo (Ed.), 1972, *Five African plays*, Femi Euba, Ferdinand Oyono, Gaston Bart-Williams, Harold Kimmel, Kwesi Kay, London, Heinemann.

Pliya, Jean, 1973, *La secrétaire particulière*, Yaoundé, CLE, collection théâtre.

Rotimi, Ola, 1971, *The Gods are not to blame*, a play, London, Oxford University Press.

Ruganda, John, 1972, *The burdens*, a play, London, Oxford University Press.

Ruganda, John, 1973, *Black mamba, Covenant with death*, two plays, Nairobi, East African Publishing House.

Salifou, André, 1973, *Tanimoune*, drame historique en sept actes, Paris, Présence Africaine.

Sekye, Kobina, (1915) 1974, *The blinkards*, a comedy, Introduction by Ayo Langley, London, Heinemann.

Senghor, Léopold Sédar, 1964a, *Poèmes*, Paris, Seuil.

Sentongo, Nuwa, 1975, 'The invisible bond', in *African plays for playing, I*, Michael Etherton (Ed.), London, Heinemann.

Sissoko, Fily Dabo, 1962, *La savane rouge*, Avignon, Presses Universelles.

Soyinka, Wole, (1963) 1974, 'The lion and the jewel', in *Collected plays 2*, London, Oxford University Press.

Soyinka, Wole, (1963) 1969, *Three short plays*, 'The swamp dwellers', 'The trials of Brother Jero', 'The strong breed', London, Oxford University Press.

Soyinka, Wole, 1963, *A dance of the forests*, a play, London, Oxford University Press.

Soyinka, Wole, 1965, *The interpreters*, a novel, London, Heinemann.

Soyinka, Wole, (1965) 1971, *The road*, a play, London, Oxford University Press.

Soyinka, Wole, 1967, *Idanre and other poems*, London, Eyre

Methuen.

Soyinka, Wole, (1967) 1973, *Kongi's harvest,* a play, London, Oxford University Press.

Soyinka, Wole, 1971, *Madmen and specialists,* a play, London, Eyre Methuen.

Soyinka, Wole, 1972, *A shuttle in the crypt,* poems, London, Rex Collings.

Soyinka, Wole, 1972, *The man died, Prison notes,* London, Rex Collings.

Soyinka, Wole, 1973, *Camwood on the leaves,* a play, London, Eyre Methuen.

Soyinka, Wole, 1975, *Death and the King's horseman,* a play, London, Eyre Methuen.

Sutherland, Efua T., 1967a, *Foriwa,* a play, Accra, State Publishing Corp.

Sutherland, Efua T., 1975, *Edufa,* a play, London, Longman.

Sutherland, Efua T., 1975, *The marriage of Anansewa,* a story-telling drama, London, Longman.

Towo-Atangana, Gaspar et Françoise, 1966, *Ndenbobo, l'araignée toiliére,* Conte beti, Yaoundé, Abbia-CLE.

Tsaro-Wiwa, Ken, 1973, 'The transistor radio', in *African Theatre,* Gwyneth Henderson (Ed.), London, Heinemann.

Tutuola, Amos, 1952, *The Palm-wine drinkard,* London, Faber and Faber.

Watene, Kenneth, 1973, *My son for my freedom, The haunting past, The broken pot,* plays, Nairobi, East African Publishing House.

Zadi Zaourou, Bernard, 1975, *Les sofas suivi de l'oeil,* Paris, Oswald, collection théâtre.

II OTHER BOOKS AND ARTICLES

Actes, *du Colloque sur le théâtre africain — 1970, 1971*, Paris, Présence Africaine.

Adedeji, J.A., 1967, 'Form and function of satire in Yoruba drama', In *Odu, A journal of African studies*, 4, (1): 71 — 72.

Adedeji, J.A., 1971, 'Oral tradition and the contemporary theatre in Nigieria', in *Research in African Literature*, 2 (2): 134 — 149.

Apronti, E.O., 1976, 'The tyranny of time. The theme of time in the artistic consciousness of South African writers', in *African Literature Today*, 8: 106 — 114.

Baal, J. van, 1967, *Mensen in verandering, Ontstaan en groei van een nieuwe cultuur in ontwikkelingslanden*, Amsterdam, Arbeidspers.

Balandier, Georges, 1965, *La vie quotidienne au royaume de Kongo du XVIe au XVIIIe siécle*, Paris, Hachette.

Bascom, W.R., 1965, 'Folklore and literature', in *The African World. A survey of social research*, R.A. Lystad (Ed.) London, Praeger,

Bebey, Francis, 1969, *Musique de l'Afrique*, Paris, Horizons de France.

Beier, Ulli, (1967) 1973, 'Yoruba theatre', in *Idem, (Ed.), Introduction to African literature. An anthology of critical writing on African and oral tradition*, London, Longman.

Beier, Ulli (Ed.), (1966) 1974, *The origin of life and death, African creation myths*, London, Heinemann.

Beiss, Adolf, 1954, *Das drama als soziologisches phänomen*, Braunschweig, Waisenhaus.

Benedict, Ruth, (1935) 1971, *Patterns of culture*, London, Routledge and Kegan Paul.

Berry, Boyd M., 1972, 'On looking at "Madmen and specialists" ', in *Pan African Journal*, 5 (4): 451 — 471.

Burns, Elizabeth, 1973, *Theatricality. A study of convention in the theatre and in social life*, New York, Harper and Row.

Colin, Roland, 1957, *Les contes de l'Ouest Africain*, Paris, Présence Africaine.

Colin, Roland, 1965, *Littérature Africaine d'hier et de demain*, Paris, ADEC.

Cornevin, Robert, 1960, *Histoire des peuples de l'Afrique noire*, Paris Berger-Levrault.

Cornevin, Robert, 1970, *Le théâtre en Afrique noire et à Madagascar*, Paris, Le livre Africain.

Dailly, Christopher, 1971, 'L'histoire comme source d'inspiration', in *Le théâtre Africain actes du colloque d'Abidjan — 1970*, Paris, Présence Africaine.

Dathorne, O.R., 1974, *The black mind. A history of African literature*, Minneapolis, University of Minnesota Press.

Delafosse, M., 1916, *Contributoin à l'étude du théâtre chez les noirs*, Annales et Mémoires Com. d'Et., AOF.

Dieterlen, Germaine, 1951, *Essai sur la religion barbara*, Paris, PUF.

Eliade, Mircea, (1957) 1972, *Mythes, rêves et mystéres*, Paris.

Ellison, R.E., 1935, 'A Bornu puppet show', in *Nigerian Field*, 4

Eno-Belinga, M.S., 1965, *Littérature et musique populaire en Afrique noire*, Toulouse, Editions Cujas.

Esslin, Martin, (1967) 1973, 'Two Nigerian playwrights: Wole Soyinka; J.P. Clark', in *Introduction to African literature*, Ulli Beier (Ed.), London, Longman.

Etherton, Michael, 1976, 'The dilemma of the popular playwright. The work of Kabwe Kasoma and V.E. Musinga', in *African literature today, 8: 26 — 41.

Fanon, Frantz, 1961, *Les damnés de la terre*, Paris, Maspéro.

Finnegan, Ruth, 1970, *Oral literature in Africa*, Oxford, Clarendon Press.

Frazer, J.G., (1922) 1974, *The golden bough. A study in magic and religion*, London, MacMillan.

Graft, J.C. de, 1976, 'Roots in African drama and theater', in

African literature today, 8: 1 — 25.

Hodgkin, Thomas. (1956) 1965, *Nationalism in colonial Africa*, London, F. Muller.

Holas, B., 1968, *Les dieux d'Afrique noire*, Paris, Paul Geuthner.

Horton, R., 1963, 'The Kalabari Ekine society: a borderland of religion and art', in *Africa, 33.*

Hunningher, B., *The origin of the theater*, Amsterdam, Qurido.

Jones, Eldred D., 1971a, 'The essential Soyinka', in *Introduction to Nigerian literature*, Bruce King (Ed.), Lagos, University of Lagos and London, Evan Borthers.

Jones, Eldred D., 1971b, 'Progress and civilization in the work of Wole Soyinka', in *Perspectives on African literature*, Christopher Heywood (Ed.), London, Heinemann.

Jones, Eldred D., 1973, *The writing of Wole Soyinka*, London, Heinemann.

Jones, Eldred D., 1976, Editorial to 'Drama in Africa', in *African literature today*, 8: VII-VIII.

Jones, G.I., 1945, 'Masked plays of South-Eastern Nigeria', in *Geographical Magazine*, 18(5).

Kaké, Ibrahima Baba, 1969, 'Signification historique de la passion de Dona Béatrice, la Jeanne d'Arc Congolaise (1704 — 1706)', in *Mélanges. Réflexions d'hommes de culture (Présence Africaine 1947 — 1967)*, Paris, Présence Africaine.

Kesteloot, Lilyan, 1971, *La poésie traditionnelle*, Paris, Nathan.

Knappert, Jan, 1958, *Het epos van Heraklios. Een proeve van Swahili poëzie*, Proefschrift Rijksuniversiteit van Leiden.

Köbben, A.J.F., 1971(2), *Van primitieven tot medeburgers*, Assen, Van Gorcum.

Labouret, H. et Travélé, M., 1928, Le théâtre mandigue (Soudan français), in *Africa, I.*

Laude, Jean, 1966, *Les arts d'Afrique noire*, Paris, Livre de poche, Librairie générale Française.

Laurence, Margaret, 1969, *Long drums and cannons. Nigerian dramatists and novelists*, New York, Washington, Fred A. Praeger.

Leeuw, G. van der, 1955, *Wegen en grenzen. Een studie over de verhouding van religie en kunst*, Amsterdam, Paris.

Lévi-Strauss, Claude, 1958, *Anthropologie structurale*, Paris, Plon.

Lévi-Strauss, Claude, 1964 — 1971, *Mythologiques I, II, III, IV*, Paris, Plon.

Little, Kenneth, 1973, *African women in towns. An aspect of Africa's social revolution*, Cambridge University Press.

Lord, Albert B., 1960, *The singer of tales*, Cambridge, Mass., Harvard University Press.

Lüthi, Max, (1947) 1974, *Das Europäische Volkmärchen*, München, Francke Verlag.

Lüthi Max, 1970, *Volksliteratur und Hochliteratur. Menschenbild, Thematik, Formstreben*, Bern/München, Francke Verlag.

Mbughuni, L.A., 1976, 'Old and new drama from East Africa', a review of the works of four contemporary dramatists: Rebecca Njau, Ebrahim Hussein, Peninah Muhando and Ngugi, in *African literature today, 8:* 85 — 98.

Memmi, Albert, 1966, *Portrait du colonisé précédé du portrait du colonisateur*, Préface de Jean-Paul Sartre, Paris, Pauvert.

Métraux, Alfred, (1959) 1972, *Voodoo in Haiti*, London, André Deutsch.

Moore, Gerald, 1971, *Wole Soyinka*, London, Evans.

Mouralis, Bernard, 1971, 'L'ecole William Ponty et la politique culturelle', in *Le théâtre négro-Africain. Actes du Colloque d'Abidjan — 1970*, Paris, Présence Africaine.

Mphahlele, Ezekiel, 1962, *The African image*, New York, Praeger.

Obiechina, Emmanuel, 1975, *Culture, tradition and society in the West African novel*, London, Cambridge University Press.

Ogumba, Oyin, 1970a en b, 'The traditional content of Wole Soyinka's plays' in *African literature today*, 4: 2 — 18; *ibid*, 5: 106 — 115.

Ogumba, Oyin, 1971, 'Modern drama in West Africa', in *Perspectives in African literature*, Christopher Heywood (Ed.), London, Heinemann.

Ogunbesan, Kolawole, 1973, 'A king for all seasons: Chaka' in African literature in *Présence Africaine, 88 (4):* 197 — 217.

Parinder, Geoffrey, 1973, *African mythology*, London, Hamlyn.

Postel-Coster, Els en Schrijvers, Joke, 1976, *Vrouwen op weg*, Assen van Gorcum.

Ricard, Alain, 1975, 'Concours et concert. Théâtre scolaire et théâtre populaire au Togo' in *Revue d'histoire du théâtre, 1:* 44 — 85.

Rop, A. de, 1964, *Lianja l'épopée des Mongo*, Bruxelels, Arsom 30 (1).

Rotimi, Ola, 1971, 'Traditional Nigerian drama' in *Introduction to Nigerian literature*, Bruce King (ed.), Lagos University of Lagos, London, Evans Brothers.

Roumain, Jacques, (1946) 1972, *Gouverneurs de la rosée*, Paris, Les éditeurs Français réunis.

Schipper, Jan, 1970, *Koloniale opinies over Kongo*, proefschrift Rijksuniversiteit van Leiden.

Schipper-de Leeuw, Mineke, 1973, *Le Blanc et l'Occident au miroir du roman négro-Africain de langue Française*, Assen/Amsterdam, Van Gorcum.

Schipper-de Leeuw, Mineke, 1976, 'Migration d'un movement: le cas de la negritude', B. Lindfors and U. Schild (Eda.), in *Neo-African literature and culture. Essays in memory of Jan Heinz Jahn*, Series Mainzer Afrika studien, Wiesbaden, Herman Verlag.

Senghor, Léopold Sédar, 1964b, *Liberté I. Négritude et humanisme*, Paris, Seuil.

Shipley, J.Th., (Ed.) 1970, *Dictionary of world literary terms*.

forms, techniques, criticism, London, Allen and Unwin.

Sonfo, Alphamoye, 1971, 'Les sources d'inspiration du théâtre Africain', in *Le théâtre négro-Africain, Actes du Colloque d'Abidjan — 1970*, Paris, Présence Africaine.

Soyinka Wole, 1966, 'Modern Negro-African threatre. The Nigerian stage. A study in tyranny and individual survival', in *Colloquium on Negro art, Vol I*, Paris, Society of African culture, Présence Africaine.

Soyinka, Wole, 1975b, 'The road from Amilcar Cabral', in the *Nigerian Daily Times*, December 1922.

Sutherland, Efua, 1972, 'Interview by Maxine Lautré' in *African writers talking*, Duerden, Dennis and Pieterse, Cosmo (eds.), London, Heinemann.

Traore, Bakary, 1958, *Le théâtre négro-Africain et ses fonctions sociales*, Paris, Présence Africaine.

Traore, Bakary, 1967, *Préface á l'xil d'Alboury et La decision de Cheik A. Ndao*, Paris, Oswald collection théâtre.

Traore, Bakary, 1970, 'Les tendances actuelles dans le théâtre Africain' in *Le théâtre négro-Africain, Acetes du Colloque d'Abidjan — 1970*, Paris, Présence Africaine.

Voltz, Piere, 1964, *La comédie*, Paris, Armand Colin.

Vries J. de, 1959, *Heldenlied en heldensage*, Utrecht/Antwerpen, Aula.